BOSTON'S
100
GREATEST
GAMERS

**Ranking the most clutch athletes in
Boston sports history**

ROB SNEDDON

 Candlepin Press

BOSTON'S 100 GREATEST GAMERS

Rob Sneddon

ISBN-13: 9781790184699

Cover and Book Design
Tammy Francoeur Sneddon
Photo Inset Illustrations by Tammy Francoeur Sneddon
Background photo ©istockphoto.com/Tammyasian

Published by Candlepin Press
Somersworth, New Hampshire

First edition, November 2018
Printed in the United States of America

In memory of my brother-in-law, Bill Bates,
a gamer if ever there was one.

TABLE OF CONTENTS

TABLE OF CONTENTS

TABLE OF CONTENTS

TABLE OF CONTENTS

INTRODUCTION

I t was sports-radio gold. Dennis Eckersley was calling WEEI's The Big Show from his car, and he was hot. "You old bastards got a lotta nerve!" Eck said. "You are beyond your f---ing age!"

This was during 'EEI's heyday, before the Red Sox won it all in 2004 and rounded the sharpest edges off the fan base. The Big Show was a roiling cauldron of vitriol, especially when it came to baseball. On this particular afternoon, former Sox shortstop Rico Petrocelli was on with cohost Dick Radatz, Rico's old teammate from the mid '60s.

Radatz held a graduate degree from the old school. A 6'6" reliever, he survived on sheer strength and endurance. No less than Mickey Mantle nicknamed him "The Monster." Once, in 1963, Radatz threw the last six innings of an extra-inning game in Baltimore to pick up the win, then threw 8⅔ innings to win another extra-inning game in Detroit just two days later.

So when Radatz expressed disdain for the modern concept of relief "specialists," he spoke with a basso profundo voice of experience. And that afternoon on The Big Show, he said that he didn't think Eckersley —a closer—should have been named American League MVP in 1992. That season Eck saved 51 games in 54 chances for the AL West champion Oakland A's. But he pitched just 80 innings.

Compare that to Radatz's best season, 1964. He won 16 games, all in relief, and also led the AL with 29 saves. And he threw 157 innings— almost twice the workload Eckersley had in '92. But The Monster finished a distant ninth in MVP voting. So when Eckersley called in to try to call him out, Radatz didn't back down, let alone apologize.

His casual defiance detonated Eck's f-bomb. And that, in turn, prompted Petrocelli to speak up. "Hey, Eck," Rico said. "C'mon over here and talk. Don't talk in the car. C,mon, pal."

"You want in on it?" Eckersley said.

"I want you to come over here," Petrocelli said. "That's what I want. We're here, right across the street from the ballpark. OK?"

"Ohh, Rico…"

"Yeah, that's me, Eck. You come over here!"

There, in a few seconds of sports-radio sound and fury, you'll find the nebulous qualities that make someone a gamer—or not. All three of those guys played for the Red Sox. Only one of them, Dennis Eckersley, is in the Hall of Fame. He's also the only one of the three who did not make the cut for this book.

That tells you something about the criteria for this list. Individual stats weren't that important. You don't paint by numbers when creating a portrait of a gamer. Much of that *gamer* quality comes down to a simple work ethic—a willingness to, as Bill Belichick famously put it, "Do your job."

Dick Radatz's job was to finish the game—which was distinct from closing it. In some cases finishing the game meant firing a quick 1-2-3 ninth. Other times that meant laboring until well past midnight. And it didn't matter that he was working overtime on behalf of Red Sox teams that were universally lousy. The Sox never had a winning record during Radatz's five years in Boston and finished no higher than seventh. They bottomed out at 62–100 in 1965, when they finished ninth.

That was Radatz's last full season in Boston. And it was Petrocelli's first. Dim as it was, the torch was passed.

The Red Sox finished ninth again in 1966 and appeared headed for another dreary season in 1967. They stood at 31–31 in late June when they headed for New York, Petrocelli's hometown, for a series with the Yankees. After taking the first game 7–1, Boston sent budding ace Jim Lonborg to the mound. It was already 4–0 Boston in the top of the second when Yankees starter Thad Tillotson hit Sox third baseman Joe Foy in the helmet with a pitch. When Tillotson batted in the last of the second (there was no DH then), Longborg drilled him between the shoulder blades. ("What do you think?" Lonborg said when asked if he'd done it on purpose.)

A horde of Yankees, led by native New Yorker Joe Pepitone, charged from the dugout. Petrocelli, who had emerged as a team leader, led the countercharge from shortstop.

Petrocelli and Pepitone were friends. And each later said his original intent was to try to use that friendship to defuse the situation. But things turned ugly—no one was sure exactly how—and a full-on brawl began. Pepitone left the game with a sore left wrist.

The message was clear. He might have been a native New Yorker, but Rico Petrocelli was a Bostonian now—and his Red Sox teammates came first. The Red Sox won the game 8–1 and went 60–39 thereafter to win their first American League pennant since 1946.

Rico's fighting spirit re-emerged that day on The Big Show. Didn't matter that Eck was a former Red Sox player and fellow media member, or that he was considerably younger and bigger than Petrocelli, or that he'd been quite a gamer himself when he played in his native Oakland.

Nope. The only thing that mattered in that moment was that Dennis Eckersley had disrespected Dick Radatz. So as far as Rico was concerned, it was *on*.

That's another hallmark of a gamer. You work hard without complaining, you get the most out of your ability, you care more about wins and losses than individual numbers—and you stand up for your teammates without a second thought.

100

Bill Mueller
Red Sox Third Baseman, 2003–2005

He was easy to overlook on a team of dirt dogs, idiots, and Manny Being Manny. Bill Mueller wasn't a character, but he was a character guy. And the 2004 Red Sox needed all the character guys they could assemble to pull off the greatest postseason turnaround in baseball history.

A switch hitter who could produce from either the top or bottom third of the order, Mueller led the American League with a .326 average in 2003. He also had power, producing a career-high 19 homers that season. But the 2003 Red Sox had six players who hit at least 25 homers.

Still, in a season in which offensive eruptions occurred with the regularity of Old Faithful, it was Mueller who put up the greatest outburst of all. He had three homers and nine RBI at Texas on July 29. Two of the homers were grand slams, in consecutive innings, from each side of the plate—making Mueller the first major leaguer ever to accomplish the feat.

And a year later, when the Red Sox won their first World Series in 86 years, who led the offense with a .429 average in sweeping the Cardinals? Bill Mueller.

Of course, before the Red Sox reached that World Series, they overcame the heavy burden of history and the New York Yankees—which were the same thing.

Two rallies against New York stood out in that turn-about season: one in which the Sox came back from a five-run deficit in July, and the other in which they rallied from a ninth-inning deficit in Game 4 of the ALCS. Mueller was instrumental in both. Even then he managed to keep a low profile. Mention those games to Sox fans today, and the two names that immediately spring to mind are Jason Varitek and Dave Roberts. Varitek provided a spark in that July comeback by stuffing his catcher's mitt in Alex Rodriguez's face—a moment immortalized on man-cave posters across New England. And with the Sox down by a run in the ninth in Game 4 of the ALCS, three outs from being swept, pinch-runner Roberts stole second to get in scoring position and set up the rally of all rallies.

But in each case the guy who produced the hit the Sox absolutely had to have was Bill Mueller. And in each case it came off the game's greatest closer, Mariano Rivera. On a rainy July Saturday Mueller homered into the bullpen, turning a 10–9 deficit into an 11–10 walkoff win. On a chilly October Sunday, he rapped a 93-mph cutter up the middle to bring Roberts home and make the most hardened hard-ball fan base suddenly believe in make-believe.

Knuckleballer Tim Wakefield—who made his own unsung contribution to the miracle of 2004 by preserving the bullpen in the Sox' 19–8 pounding in Game 3—recognized how vital Mueller was. "It was a team full of 'gamers,' " Wakefield later told the *Globe*'s Bob Ryan. "And he was at the top of the list."

Bad knees plagued Mueller, who played just three years in Boston. He signed with the Dodgers after the 2005 season but played only 32 games before yet another knee surgery led him to retire.

99

Isaiah Thomas
Celtics Guard, 2015–2017

*W*e need a reliable fourth-quarter scorer who's not afraid to take the ball to the basket and get to the line. So let's trade a first-round pick for a 5'9" guard who was the last pick in the NBA draft.

Brilliant!

No, seriously. That *was* brilliant.

Over the summer of 2013, the Celtics dismantled the last of the Doc Rivers, Ubuntu, Big-Three-2.0 team. President of basketball operations Danny Ainge needed to perform another extreme makeover. His first move was to replace Rivers with 36-year-old Brad Stevens, who came to the NBA from plucky Butler, a perennial March Madness overachiever.

Step two was to try to rebuild through the draft. No one really cared that the 2013–14 Celtics finished 25–57. They were just playing the lottery anyway. But the Ping-Pong balls failed to bounce their way. Then the 2014–15 Celtics started 20–31 and sat tenth in the Eastern Conference at the All-Star break.

So they acquired Isaiah Thomas from Phoenix at the trade deadline. "Isaiah is a big personality," said Ainge, "and I think as he matures he has the potential to be a great leader."

The Celtics finished that season 20–11 and made the playoffs. They've been on a steady upward trajectory ever since. And while it's oversimplifying things to say that Isaiah Thomas was solely responsible for turning the franchise around, he was certainly a catalyst.

He was the ideal leader for a group of underdogs trying to overthrow

King James in the Eastern Conference. He was fueled by slights. ("Pick Me Last Again.") He didn't shrink from the big moment—he sought it. "I love the fourth quarter," Thomas said. "I love when the game is close. I want to be that type of guy."

Thomas clearly established himself as *that guy* for the Celtics. There was his 42-point effort in bringing the Celtics their first playoff win in three years. His 44 points on just 16 shots in a gritty road win over a tough Memphis team in December 2016. His 29-point fourth-quarter explosion against Miami a little more than a week later. No Celtic—neither Jones nor Heinsohn nor Havlicek nor Cowens nor Bird nor McHale nor Pierce nor Allen—ever scored more points in a quarter.

But his grittiest performance came in Game 2 of the 2017 Eastern Conference Semifinals against the Washington Wizards. Playing on what would have been his late sister Chyna's 23rd birthday—just 17 days after she was killed in a car accident in their home state of Washington—and recovering from dental surgery after having had a tooth knocked out in Game 1, as well as a lingering hip injury that eventually sidelined him in the Eastern Conference Finals, Thomas went off for 53 points in the Celtics' 129–119 overtime win. Said coach Brad Stevens afterward, "What he's done in the last two weeks has been remarkable."

It was a fitting coda for a remarkable two years.

Thomas was as shocked as anyone by the trade that sent him to Cleveland for Kyrie Irving in August 2017. As he wrote in The Players' Tribune, *"Man, man, am I going to miss this city. Man, am I going to miss being a Celtic." Yes, he got the whole Boston thing. "It's almost like me and the city, my Celtics teams and these Celtic fans, we both shared the same heart, that same mentality. We both just wanted to win—now. ... It was like, Man, f--- the lottery."*

98

Dave Henderson
Red Sox Outfielder, 1986–1987

He came to Boston a generation too soon. With his easy laugh and imperviousness to pressure, Dave Henderson would have been a good fit on the reverse-the-curse Red Sox of 2004. Instead, he ran counter to the bad karma on the coulda-woulda-shoulda Red Sox of 1986.

No one expected postseason heroics from Dave Henderson. He came from Seattle in a midseason trade to shore up the outfield. Any big October moments would certainly involve Cy Young favorite Roger Clemens (24–4) or a potent offense that featured future Hall of Famers Jim Rice and Wade Boggs, along with Don Baylor (31 homers) and Dwight Evans (26 homers). Henderson's best bet to distinguish himself would be with a game-saving catch. He had hit just .196 with one home run that season.

But instead of a great defensive play, Henderson made a hideous gaffe. The Red Sox trailed the Angels 3–1 in the best-of-seven American League Championship Series but had a 2–1 lead in Game 5. In the last of the sixth, Henderson—who was in the game only because center-fielder Tony Armas had left with an injury—sprinted back after a one-on, two-out drive from Angels first baseman Bobby Grich. Henderson leaped for the ball. But instead of snagging it for a run-saving catch, he knocked it over the wall for a two-run homer.

By the ninth, the Angels had extended their lead to 5–2. Don Baylor closed the gap with a two-run homer. Then, with two outs, catcher Rich Gedman was hit by a pitch to put the tying run on. Guess who was up next?

It seemed the rally was destined to make Dave Henderson feel worse. That home run he'd gifted the Angels was now the difference in the game. And now, batting against Angels closer Donnie Moore, Henderson was in position to make the last out. Instead he made himself an instant hero across New England by swatting a Moore forkball over the wall in left to put the Sox ahead 6–5.

The Angels tied it in the home half of the ninth. It stayed that way until the 11th, when Henderson drove home the decisive run with a sacrifice fly.

That last-gasp homer was Henderson's only hit of the series. But it was enough to kick-start a comeback for the ages that put the Red Sox into the World Series against the Mets.

With Armas out, Henderson came up huge against New York. He hit .400 in the World Series with a pair of home runs. The second was a solo shot leading off the tenth in Game 6 at Shea Stadium, with the Sox up three games to two. Henderson's blast put Boston up 4–3 and an insurance run made it 5–3. That left the Sox just three outs from their first World Series title since 1918. And then. …

No need to rehash the grisly autopsy. It's enough to say that, had the Red Sox held on, Dave Henderson would have been as celebrated in Boston in 1986 as Dave Roberts was in 2004.

Less than a year after his epic October, Henderson was traded to San Francisco. He then signed as a free agent with Oakland, where he won a World Series in 1989. In December 2015 he died of a heart attack just three months after a kidney transplant. He was 57. "He was so much fun to be around," former teammate Jim Rice told the Boston Globe. *"And he played the game like he was a kid."*

97

Gino Cappelletti
Patriots Placekicker, Defensive Back, and Slot Receiver, 1960–1970

Sometimes you just have to stick with it. Take Gino Cappelletti. When Cappelletti failed to make the Detroit Lions as an undrafted free agent in 1955, his pro football prospects appeared dim. But the former University of Minnesota quarterback took his talents to Canada, where he kept his dream on life support. Sandwiched around a hitch in the U.S. Army, Cappelletti toiled for the Ontario Rugby Football Union's Toronto Balmy Beach club and the CFL's Saskatchewan Rough Riders, among other outfits.

Finally, after five years as a football vagabond, Cappelletti took a shot at a new venture. In 1960 he signed with the American Football League's Boston Patriots. He ended up playing in every one of the team's 142 games.

Cappelletti embodied "The Patriot Way" long before it was called that. He was versatile. As a placekicker, he scored the first points in AFL history, on a 35-yard field goal on a warm Friday night at Nickerson Field. He also played defensive back during the Pats' inaugural season—and did it well enough to pick off Raiders quarterback Tom Flores three times in one game.

The next season Cappelletti switched to receiver and caught eight touchdown passes. (He also threw one, on the only pass attempt of his career.) He became a Patriots archetype: the gritty slot receiver—or flanker, as it was called then—that other teams overlooked.

In 1964, Cappelletti set a career high with 49 receptions, including seven for touchdowns. He also kicked 25 field goals and was named AFL Player of the Year.

That December *Sports Illustrated*'s Bud Shrake summed up Cappelletti's canny effectiveness: "At the University of Minnesota he was called 'Gino the Snail.' He is small and slow. Defensive backs tend to think of him primarily as a field-goal kicker and they relax on him. When they do, Cappelletti uses a few of his shrewd fakes and is gone."

1970, Cappelletti's final season, was the first season of pro football's mega merger. The AFL became the AFC. It had taken 15 years since that failed tryout in Detroit, but Gino Cappelletti had finally made the NFL. And he'd brought the city of Boston along with him.

Cappelletti enjoyed an even longer second career as a Patriots radio analyst. He worked in the booth for 32 seasons, including 28 alongside Gil Santos. He was inducted into the Patriots Hall of Fame in 1992 and had his jersey number, 20, retired.

96

Tris Speaker
Red Sox Centerfielder, 1907–1915

He delivered the first walk-off hit in Fenway Park history, a sharp opposite-field single past shortstop that brought in the winning run in the last of the eleventh as the Red Sox beat the New York Highlanders (soon to be renamed the Yankees) 7–6 on Opening Day, 1912.

A slow but steady courtship between the Red Sox and their prickly centerfielder from Texas blossomed into a brief but beautiful marriage.

The Sox didn't want Speaker at first. After he hit just .158 in a late stint with the team in 1907, they declined to invite him back. But he returned anyway, paying his own way to Spring Training in Arkansas in 1908. As an additional indignity, the Red Sox ended up selling him to a minor league team in Little Rock in exchange for use of the team's facilities.

Despite this inauspicious start, Speaker turned himself into a major leaguer, first by focusing on his outfield play. A pioneer in the art of defensive positioning, Speaker played center the way some Little Leaguers do today, at such a shallow depth that he occasionally turned unassisted double plays at second base.

It took his offense a while to catch up with his defense. But when he finally made the Sox full time in 1909, he became a .300 hitter. He also had what passed for good power in the dead-ball era, with 22 home runs in his first three seasons.

Still, no one was prepared for the energizing effect that Boston's new ballpark would have on the Red Sox in general, and Tris Speaker in particular. A team that had finished fifth, 24 games back, in 1911 erupted in 1912. The Red Sox finished 105–47, including 57–20 at Fenway Park. They won the American League pennant by a staggering 14 games.

And Speaker was the spark plug. He hit .383 and led the league in doubles, home runs, and OBP. He was named MVP, and then contributed a key hit in the Sox' tenth-inning rally to beat the Giants in the deciding game of the 1912 World Series.

Over the next three seasons, Speaker averaged 150 games in center and led the Red Sox to another World Series triumph, in 1915. He then became an unfortunate archetype—the fan favorite who leaves town because Red Sox management makes a hideous misjudgment. (See Ruth, George Herman and Fisk, Carlton Ernest). When Sox ownership asked Speaker to take a 50% pay cut because his average had dipped all the way down to .322 (The slacker!), Speaker held out. So the Sox dealt him to a dreadful Cleveland Indians team. "I am mighty sorry to leave Boston because I have been treated royally here [and] I have come to regard Boston as my second home," Speaker said. "I don't want to leave, but neither do I want to stay on a ball team where I am not wanted by the management."

The Sox' assessment of Speaker's "decline" proved to be hasty indeed. He led the AL in seven offensive categories in 1916, including batting average (.386). Over 11 seasons with the Indians, he hit .354 and led Cleveland to its first World Series title, in 1920. Speaker was inducted into the Hall of Fame in 1937 and later named to Major League Baseball's All-Century Team.

95

Francis Ouimet
1913 U.S. Open Winner

The Country Club isn't in the country anymore. Suburban Boston has enveloped Brookline, including the house at 246 Clyde Street where young Francis Ouimet first glimpsed the game of golf in 1897. He could hardly have avoided it; his second-story bedroom looked out on the Country Club's 17th hole.

Francis was the son of a working-class immigrant. The Country Club was a playground for Boston Brahmans. Yet simple proximity provided an entrée. By age nine Francis was a caddie. And as he later wrote, "I can remember well how I used to awaken at 4:00 a.m. and run over to the club and play in my bare feet before anyone was astir."

By age 20 he was the state's top amateur.

In September 1913 the Country Club hosted the U.S. Open, which featured Britain's Harry Vardon and Ted Ray, two of the best in the world. But Golf was still a fringe spectator sport in America. So USGA president Robert Watson invited Ouimet to participate. Maybe having a local kid involved would boost interest.

Ouimet, still an amateur, had to juggle his work schedule at a sporting goods store to accommodate Watson's request. The first day's play—36 holes—drew about 2,500 spectators, including former President William Howard Taft. As expected, Vardon won. But just one stroke behind him was Ouimet, who actually led the round for much of the day. "After the spectators heard at the conclusion of the first 18 holes that Francis Ouimet, the only amateur who had made any kind of a showing, was leading the field by a stroke," the *Boston Globe* reported, "the Woodland player was followed by at least 700 persons in his afternoon's play, a large majority leaving Vardon."

Mission accomplished. The local kid had goosed interest in golf. Still, no one expected him to still be in the hunt after Day 4.

But there he was. And he surged in shocking fashion, making up a four-stroke deficit to tie Vardon and Ray and force an 18-hole play-off. To make the story even more newspaper-ready, his caddie was a spunky ten-year-old named Eddie Lowery, who was barely taller than the bag he was lugging. The thrilling, improbable finish sparked "the most enthusiastic demonstration ever accorded a golfer in this country or probably in the world," gushed the *Globe*'s John G. Anderson.

The next day, before the playoff, Lowery—displaying a patriotic ribbon on his lapel—gave Ouimet a pep talk. "You've just got to beat those fellows, Francis," the young caddie said. "They can never take the championship across the water with them!"

Suitably inspired, Ouimet went out and won by five strokes. The coup de grace was a birdie on the 17th hole—the one right outside his bedroom window.

Ouimet was humble in victory. Young Lowery was less so. "Those Englishmen gave me the laugh at first because I was so small," he said, "but after the match was finished and Francis was the winner, the first thing I did was turn around and give *them* the laugh."

Ouimet's astonishing upset is credited with spiking interest in golf nation-wide, with participation increasing six-fold over the next decade. Ouimet never did turn pro, but he continued to play at a high level. Among other noteworthy achievements, he won a pair of U.S. Amateurs 17 years apart (1914 and 1931). He became a successful businessman and remained a key figure in Boston sports for the rest of his life. Since 1949 a scholarship fund bearing his name has awarded more than $26 million in assistance to college students who had worked at Massachusetts golf courses. Ouimet died in Newton, Massachusetts, in 1967. In 2005 Disney released a film about the 1913 U.S. Open, The Greatest Game Ever Played, which writer Mark Frost adapted from his own bestselling book.

94

Dick Radatz
Red Sox Pitcher, 1962–1966

Had Dick Radatz pitched today, he might have been one of the best closers ever. He certainly had the right mentality. When Radatz came on in the ninth, former Sox starter Bill Monbouquette once recalled, "He'd say, 'Go in the clubhouse, crack me a Bud, and I'll be right up.' And he would."

At 6'6" and 230 pounds, Radatz relied strictly on high-octane gas. "He had no off-speed pitch," Monbouquette said. "He'd come right at you, get you 0-and-2, and just blow you away. He was a pure power guy."

It's hard for a pitcher to sustain that approach for nine innings. That's probably why Radatz developed arm trouble as a starter in the minor leagues. Johnny Pesky, who was then the manager of Boston's top affiliate, the Seattle Rainiers, converted him to a reliever.

As a rookie in 1962, Radatz led the American League in appearances, with 62, and saves, with 24. He allowed no earned runs through his first 12 outings.

Radatz's workload during those first dozen games ranged from just a third of an inning to 3⅓. That set the tone for his career. Back then there were no closers per se, let alone setup men or middle relievers. A team's best bullpen pitcher was called a "fireman." Managers would use him to extinguish a rally whenever it flared up, often as early as the sixth inning. And once he was in the game, a fireman was expected to stay out there as long as necessary.

Radatz learned that the hard way at Yankee Stadium in September of his rookie year. It was the second game of a doubleheader. Radatz came on in the bottom of the seventh with the Sox up 4–3. He got two quick outs, but then the Yankees scratched out the tying run.

Radatz stayed in the game for nine full innings before the Sox pushed across the winning run.

During his four-plus years in Boston, Radatz compiled a record of 49–34, with 102 saves. In all but 26 of those saves, he logged more than an inning.

Radatz made the All-Star Game twice. In the 1963 edition he pitched two innings and struck out five National Leaguers, including future Hall of Famers Willie Mays, Willie McCovey, and Duke Snider.

Despite his old-school pedigree, Radatz was ahead of his time. He pitched in 381 games during his major league career without making a single start—a rarity in those days. He became the first pitcher to record back-to-back seasons with at least 20 saves—then added two more 20-save seasons to the streak. And he introduced a little showmanship to the closer's role, thrusting both arms skyward after a game-ending punch-out.

But Radatz wasn't a closer. He was a fireman.

The term fit. On a succession of terrible Boston teams, Dick Radatz did his job like a dedicated civil servant.

By 1965 Radatz's velocity had dropped—little surprise, given his workload. The Red Sox traded him to Cleveland in 1966. He recorded just 18 more saves before ending his career with the Montreal Expos in 1969. Radatz eventually resettled in the Boston area and remained active both as a member of the media and a minor-league instructor. He died in 2005 after falling down a flight of stairs at his home in Easton.

93

Rico Petrocelli
Red Sox Infielder, 1963; 1965–1976

He was an accidental shortstop. Growing up in Brooklyn, Rico Petrocelli starred as a high school pitcher and outfielder. Major league scouts loved him. Then he hurt his elbow and reinvented himself as a shortstop. Most scouts fell out of love. But among the teams still interested were the hometown Yankees—and the Red Sox. Boston scout Bots Nekola got the inside track by attending Petrocelli's Sheepshead Bay High School graduation. "He took my parents and two of my brothers to dinner," Petrocelli said.

And that's pretty much all it took for the Red Sox to win Rico's loyalty.

Petrocelli was a fielding whiz from day one. At the start of his first full season, in 1965, the *Boston Globe*'s Bud Collins anointed him "possibly the best shortstop the Red Sox have ever employed." Collins also noted that in recent years, "numerous Red Sox have treated defense as something below their dignity."

But defensive wizardry carries a team only so far. As a rookie, Petrocelli hit just .232 with 13 home runs and 33 RBI. The Red Sox lost 100 games.

So Petrocelli worked on becoming a major league hitter, using the same doggedness with which he had willed himself into a major league shortstop. By 1969 he was flirting with a .300 average and 100 RBI—and he became the first shortstop in major league history to hit 40 home runs in a season. His response after belting his landmark homer against the Washington Senators at RFK Stadium on September 29? "Sorry I didn't get it in Boston."

By then Petrocelli was also a two-time All-Star, and had been a key cog in the 1967 Impossible Dream season. The scrappy Sox pushed the heavily favored Cardinals to seven games—in part because of Petrocelli's two home runs in Game 6.

Late in his career, Petrocelli hit .308 in the epic '75 World Series against the Cincinnati Reds. By then he was playing third, having volunteered to move from short in 1971 to make room for Luis Aparicio, the most dominant defensive shortstop of the era. Said Sox first base coach Don Lenhardt, noting how hard Rico worked in spring training to make the transition, "If everyone had his attitude, we could forget any trouble."

The mutual love affair between Rico and the Red Sox ended abruptly in March 1977. Petrocelli had struggled with injuries throughout the '76 season and the Red Sox had an up-and-coming third baseman, Butch Hobson, stuck behind him. So the Red Sox released Rico Petrocelli, perennial fan favorite. Those fans reacted with outrage— some even going so far as to issue death threats against manager Don Zimmer.

Rico handled his release with class. He said he understood the decision and he wished the Red Sox well. He added, "I wish my fans would stop this ridiculous thing of threatening Don Zimmer's life. I'd like to impress on these people that baseball is only a game. These decisions on which players to keep aren't easy."

Even when he was no longer part of the team, Rico Petrocelli remained a team player.

When his playing days ended Rico went over to the dark side. He wrote a column for the Boston Herald *and became a fixture on sports radio. (The transplanted New Yorker further enhanced his New England cred by hosting* Candlepins for Cash *for four years.) In 1992 he was named manager of the Pawtucket Red Sox—replacing, ironically, Butch Hobson. He was inducted into the Red Sox Hall of Fame in 1997.*

92

Malcolm Butler
Patriots Cornerback, 2014–2017

"Everyone thought I was going to be a one-hit wonder," Malcolm Butler once told *Sports Illustrated*. Ten months had passed since Butler had made the most famous interception in NFL history, to preserve the Patriots' 28–24 victory over the Seattle Seahawks in Super Bowl XLIX.

But Butler hasn't done the fade route. A season after saving the Super Bowl, he wound up in the Pro Bowl. That distinguished him from a long list of obscure players who happened to come up with the performance of their lives on the brightest stage in American sports. Like Jets cornerback Randy Beverly, whose two end-zone interceptions thwarted the Colts in a landscape-altering upset in Super Bowl III. Or Redskins running back Timmy Smith, who started just nine games in his NFL career but rushed for 204 yards in Super Bowl XXII. Or, in the most notorious example from a Patriots perspective, David Tyree. Tyree's spectacular "helmet catch," which helped Eli Manning and the Giants end the Pats' bid for a perfect season in Super Bowl XLII, was the final reception of an otherwise undistinguished career.

Butler could have been content to parlay that one brilliant play into a nice little nest egg. But he wasn't. In fact, what came next was a more pressure-packed situation than the one Butler had faced in the Super Bowl. Before his epic pick, Butler was merely an undrafted free agent from West Alabama. He had a low profile—and therefore low expectations.

That abruptly changed when the Patriots decided to let starting cornerbacks Darrelle Revis and Brandon Browner walk away following the Super Bowl. Suddenly Malcolm Butler was next man up on the depth chart.

Making one well-timed pick in the Super Bowl was one thing. But shutting down the opponent's star receiver every week? That was something else. Butler turned out to be something else, too. He made the Pro Bowl after the 2015 season, his first as a starter, when he was on the field for all but 12 possible snaps. He might have been the only one who wasn't surprised that he could perform at a high level over the long haul. Said Butler, "I guess my standards are real high."

He maintained his high standards the following year, as he again started every game in helping lead the Patriots to another white-knuckle Super Bowl victory, this time over the Falcons. And while his performance against Atlanta was the inverse of his performance against Seattle—this time his play was forgettable even though he was on the field for every defensive snap—Butler said the end result was the same. "It feels just as great," he said.

A year later, Malcolm Butler was again a pivotal figure in the Super Bowl—even though he didn't play a single down at defensive back. Bill Belichick's decision to bench him, combined with the inability of the Patriots defense to stop the Eagles in a 41–33 defeat, became the dominant offseason story. In March Butler signed a five-year, $61 million deal with the Tennessee Titans.

91

Don Nelson
Celtics Forward, 1965–1976

Bill Russell once called him the epitome of what it means to be a Celtic. For Don Nelson, going to the scorer's table was the equivalent of punching in for work. During his 11 seasons in Boston, the Celtics played 1,028 games, playoffs included. Nelson missed just 22 of them.

Red Auerbach acquired him on waivers from the Lakers in October 1965. It was a typical Auerbach move—and it summed up the difference between the Celtics and Lakers in the 1960s. Nelson, who had transformed from a post-up player at the University of Iowa to a perimeter shooter in the pros, had trouble getting shots in LA's star-studded lineup.

But Nelson could do other things, like rebound and play defense. He understood the importance of positioning. "He had all the speed and agility of an average mailbox," the *Boston Globe*'s Bob Ryan once wrote. "But he was a great team basketball player."

Auerbach recognized this. (So did the Lakers' star guard, Jerry West, who later wrote that he was surprised LA let Nelson go.) Auerbach had pioneered the "sixth man" concept, and Nelson was perfectly suited for that role. "I can put him into a game and know he'll hold the status quo," Red said. "I know some of my guys always thought he battled them when he was with the Lakers."

Fast-forward six months. With Nelson now battling for the Celtics, Boston outlasted LA to win the NBA championship in seven games. Nelson was a part of two more Finals wins over LA, including a seven-game classic in 1969, Russell's swan song. Nelson made the critical play in Game 7 at LA, grabbing a loose ball and hitting a foul-line jumper with just over a minute to play. That made it a two-possession game and thwarted a furious Lakers rally.

That shot, which bounced straight up from the back of the rim and down through the net, was also vintage Nelson. It looked awkward, but it did the job. Nelson had a funky set shot and unique free-throw form. He looked like he was trying to avoid stepping in a puddle as he pushed the ball with one hand. But Nelson didn't care about style points, just basketball points. He once led the NBA in field-goal percentage. He shot 77% from the line during his time in Boston.

Whatever the Celtics needed, Nelson provided. Once, when pressed into service as a starter in 1970, Nelson set a career high with 36 points. He topped that three games later when he went for 40 against the Rockets. And it wasn't garbage-time padding; Nelson sparked a come-from-behind victory in which the Celtics scored 54 fourth-quarter points, an NBA record at the time.

But it was the little things, the stuff not recorded in the box score, that best defined Don Nelson. Example: Nelson scored just four points in perhaps the greatest NBA game ever played, the Celtics' triple-overtime win over Phoenix in Game 5 of the 1976 NBA Finals. But it was his outlet pass that led to the layup that finally put the Celtics ahead to stay.

Boston clinched in Game 6. That was Don Nelson's last game. He ended his Celtics career as he had begun: with a championship. As Ryan wrote upon Nelson's retirement, "The triumph of ingenuity over raw talent that Don Nelson represented has almost no parallel in any professional sport."

Given Nelson's basketball ingenuity, it was logical that he became a coach. In 31 seasons with the Bucks, Warriors, Knicks, and Mavs, he won 1,335 regular-season games, the most of any coach in NBA history. He was inducted into the Naismith Memorial Basketball Hall of Fame in 2012.

90

Bobbi Gibb
Boston Marathon Pioneer

Cambridge native Bobbi Gibb didn't think of herself as a pioneer—at least not at first. In 1966, when Gibb became the first woman to file an entry for the Boston Marathon, it never occurred to her that the Boston Athletic Association would turn her down. But the BAA rejected Gibb's application on the grounds that women were "physiologically unable to run marathon distances."

"I was stunned," Gibb later wrote. "At that moment I knew that I was running for much more than my own personal challenge. I was running to change the way people think."

The way people thought about female athletes a mere half-century ago is astonishing in hindsight. At that time, the longest AAU-sanctioned event for women was a mile and a half.

A mile and a half.

Bobbi Gibb ran farther than that just to warm up. She had been running greater and greater distances—up to 40 miles—since she had first glimpsed the Marathon in 1964, while running with her dogs in the woods of suburban Boston. She wanted to be a part of it. "I didn't know the Marathon was closed to women," she wrote, "and I set about training in nurses' shoes with no instructions, no coach, and no books."

In 1966, at age 23, Gibb was ready for the Boston Marathon—even if the Boston Marathon wasn't ready for her. She decided to crash the race and run without a number, as an unofficial entrant. Wearing a hooded sweatshirt to try to conceal her gender, she hid in the bushes near the starting line and joined the middle of the pack to try to blend in.

It didn't take the other runners long to see through the ruse. To Gibb's relief, her fellow marathoners not only made no attempt to stop her—they actually encouraged her. "Contrary to what some people think," she later recalled, "it was not a men-versus-women confrontation. The men were glad that I was running. They said, 'It's a free road. We won't let anyone throw you out.'"

The impression that Gibb's history-making run stirred a controversy probably owes to a famous photo taken a year later, when a Syracuse University student named Kathrine Switzer, who had been inspired by Gibb, filed an entry under the gender-ambiguous name "K. V. Switzer" and was issued an official number bib. When someone pointed Switzer out to race co-director Jock Semple early in the running, he stormed onto the course and tried—unsuccessfully—to tear the bib off. Photographer Harry Trask captured the moment.

In fact, the general public, politicians (Massachusetts Governor John Volpe congratulated Gibb at the finish line) and the mainstream press reacted positively to her historic 1966 run—even if the tone was condescending at times. HUB BRIDE FIRST GAL TO RUN MARATHON, read the headline in the next day's Boston *Record American*.

But at least it was a start toward a more enlightened perception of women athletes. And who knows how much longer that start would have been delayed if not for Bobbi Gibb.

Unofficially, Gibb finished 125th in a field of 415 at the 1966 Boston Marathon. She also ran the Marathon in 1967 and 1968, each time finishing first among a growing, if still off-the-record, field of women. The BAA created an official women's division in 1972. In 1996 the Boston Athletic Association retroactively recognized Gibb's accomplishments, and 2016 women's winner Atsede Baysa marked the 50th anniversary of Gibb's barrier-breaking achievement by giving Gibb the champion's trophy. "I want to dedicate this trophy to her because she's an amazing woman," Baysa, a native Ethiopian, said through a translator.

89

Dick Hoyt
Boston Marathon Icon

Due respect to native New Englanders Bill Rodgers, who won four Boston Marathons, and intrepid John Kelley, who ran the race 61 times. But, hands down, the marathoner who won New England over like no other was Dick Hoyt.

Strip the sports component from this story and it is no less inspiring. In 1962 Dick and Judy Hoyt had a son, Rick. He was a spastic quadriplegic born with cerebral palsy. That diagnosis, at that time, meant no hope and no help. Rick would spend his life in an institution, unable to communicate.

The Hoyts didn't buy it. They saw the life in Rick's eyes. Together they forced others to see it, too. They ignored barriers, worked around them, or demanded that they be removed. They fought to place Rick in public schools. They worked with biomedical engineers at Tufts University to develop the Hope Machine, a device that allowed Rick to spell out messages by touching a switch with his head. Rick's first message: "Go Bruins!"

Eventually Rick graduated from Boston University. But it was in 1977, when he was a student at Westfield Middle School, that that hopeless kid made his most transformative discovery. A college lacrosse player had suffered a paralyzing injury. Supporters organized a five-mile road race as a fundraiser. Rick had a thought: If he participated in the race, he would not only raise money but could also raise the kid's spirits. Rick could show him, as perhaps no one else could, that loss of function did not equate to loss of life. So Rick asked Dick to push him the length of the racecourse in a wheelchair.

Dick had been an outstanding athlete at North Reading High. But 20 years had passed. Now he was a 37-year-old captain in the Air National Guard who hadn't jogged more than a mile in forever. Still, he ran the full five miles, pushing his son in a wheelchair that wanted to go every direction but straight. Dick was exhausted when it was over, and glad he would never have to do it again.

And then he read a message on Rick's computer monitor: "Dad, when I'm running, it feels like I'm not handicapped."

No fiery speech from a head coach ever galvanized Dick Hoyt the way that single silent sentence on a computer screen did. If running allowed Rick to transcend his disability, then Dick would transcend any obstacle to make it happen.

There were plenty. Still, within a mere four years, Team Hoyt progressed from competing in a local fundraiser to running America's most famous distance race, the Boston Marathon. But the Marathon didn't know what to do with them. They met the criteria of neither an able-bodied runner nor a wheelchair competitor. So the Hoyts ran as "bandits." Then, in 1982, Team Hoyt gained official entry to the Boston Marathon by way of the Marine Corps Marathon in D.C., meeting the stringent requirement that the Hoyts' time meet the qualifying standard for Rick's age bracket, not Dick's.

Excelsior. Team Hoyt became a fixture at the Boston Marathon for three decades, and competed in triathlons as well. (First Dick had to learn to swim, then figure out how to tow Rick in a dinghy.)

The 2013 Boston Marathon was to have been Dick Hoyt's last. But when the horrific terrorist bombing prevented Team Hoyt and thousands of other from reaching the finish line that year, Dick vowed to return in 2014 and go the distance, at age 73.

He did, of course. In so doing, Dick Hoyt ended his marathon run of Marathons the way he had started: on *his* terms.

At the end of Dick Hoyt's autobiography, Devoted: The Story of a Father's Love for His Son, *there is a letter from Rick in which he thanks Dick for a lifetime of memories "all created because you didn't give up on me."*

88

Tim Wakefield
Red Sox Pitcher, 1995–2011

He was often a janitor on the mound, cleaning up a mess. Every team needs that in the course of a 162-game season. In fact, it was that maintenance-man mentality that had brought Tim Wakefield to Boston in the first place. With the Red Sox' rotation decimated by injuries early in the 1995 season, they called up their 28-year-old knuckleball pitcher from Pawtucket. They weren't sure what they were going to get. Would it be the guy who had been named National League Rookie Pitcher of the Year in 1992, the year he won a couple of games for the Pirates in the NLCS? Or the guy who had been shelled at Triple A Buffalo in 1994? Such were the vagaries of the knuckleballer. But it almost didn't matter. The Sox just needed *innings*.

Tim Wakefield ended up giving them 3,006 innings over the next 17 seasons.

Not all of them were pretty. Wakefield's only appearances on the AL leader board were all in negative categories: 15 losses in 1997, 35 home runs allowed in 2005, a couple of seasons when he led the league in hit batsmen.

But there were also long stretches when Wakefield's knuckler was diabolical, and he was almost unhittable. It started in that '95 season; Wakefield won his first four starts—the second coming on just two days' rest—with a 0.54 ERA. He went at least seven innings in each of those starts, including a ten-inning complete game. Over that summer of '95 Wakefield helped undo damage from the recent work stoppage by giving Sox fans an old-school underdog knuckleballer to root for.

The 2007 regular season was Wakefield's most valuable. He turned 41 on August 2—and celebrated his birthday by beating the Orioles. It was one of his 17 wins that year, matching a career high, as the Red Sox went on to win the World Series.

But Wakefield didn't pitch in the '07 World Series. He had a lingering shoulder ailment, and the Red Sox made the tough decision to leave him off the roster. Wakefield, as always, handled it with class: "I just don't think it's fair to the other 24 guys on this team that I go out there and maybe I pitch well and maybe I don't."

That was his m.o. from the start: whatever was best for the team.

That's how it was in 1999, when Tom Gordon was injured and Jimy Williams made Wakefield the world's least-likely closer. He ended up with 15 saves. That's how it was in the 2003 ALCS. Wakefield had beaten the Yankees twice in two starts. Then, in Game 7, he was into his second inning of relief in the 11th when Aaron Boone ended things with a walk-off homer. Wakefield feared he would live forever in Red Sox infamy.

That didn't happen, of course. Sox fans blamed Grady Little for putting Wakefield in a position he shouldn't have been in to start with.

A year later, again facing the Yankees in extra innings with the Sox facing elimination in Game 5, Wakefield got the win with three scoreless (if precarious) innings before David Ortiz ended things in the last of the 14th.

And that relief stint had come two days after the Yankees had clubbed the Sox 19–8 to up 3–0 in the ALCS. It was one of the most notorious messes in Sox history, and Wakefield volunteered to help clean it up. He sacrificed his scheduled Game 4 start and saved the Sox bullpen with three innings of middle relief. Thanks to that thankless janitorial endeavor, the Red Sox were in position to undo 86 years of frustration in just 11 days.

Wakefield got his 200th, and last, major league win against Toronto on September 13, 2011. It was a remarkable milestone for a former first baseman who had converted to a knuckleball pitcher in the minors out of desperation, saying, "I just want to be able to say I tried everything I could to make it."

87

Steve Grogan
Patriots Quarterback, 1975–1990

His name, scattered throughout the Patriots record book, is like one of those half-smiling emoticons that denotes ambivalence. *Steve Grogan.* When longtime Pats fans see that name, they can't help but recall scores of pleasant memories—along with some vivid nightmares.

Grogan, a quarterback from the Flint Hills of Kansas, brought a flinty disposition to a team that desperately needed it. He arrived in 1975; the Patriots hadn't had a winning season since 1964.

Grogan is listed among New England's all-time top three in games played, in pass attempts, in passing yards, in passing touchdowns, and in 300-yard passing games.

He also ranks among the top 20 in rushing yards, and he's fourth in rushing touchdowns with 35.

Twelve of Grogan's rushing TDs came in a single season, 1976. That stood as an NFL record for a quarterback until Cam Newton came along in 2011.

In 1978 Grogan ran for 539 yards, one of four Pats runners to top 500 yards that year. The '78 Pats set a single-season NFL rushing record of 3,156 yards that still stands.

Grogan was also the first QB to lead the Patriots to an 11-win season (in 1976), and the only quarterback other than Tom Brady to lead the team to five straight winning seasons.

But Grogan is also the franchise leader in interceptions (with 208). And he is New England's all-time (if unofficial) leader in starting jobs lost and regained (Tony Eason and Marc Wilson were among those who replaced him), and in medical procedures—an inevitable side effect for a QB who was always willing to pull the ball down and try to make something out of nothing. And there was no sliding in those days. "I tried to play like I was a football player and not just a quarterback," Grogan once said. "If I had to deliver a blow, I'd deliver a blow. If I had to run and take the hit, I'd take the hit."

He paid the price for those hits. He broke his left leg twice. He had five knee surgeries, two ruptured disks in his neck, a broken hand, multiple separated shoulders (both sides) and at least three concussions. ("I don't remember the third quarter," he said after one game.)

Said former Pats tight end Don Hasselbeck (father of Matt and Tim), "Steve Grogan is the toughest football player I ever played with. You know how he's had all those operations? Well, he was awake for every one of them. He wanted to watch. I asked him about the last one, when they had to put a couple of pins in him, and he said that one was a little tougher than the others because he could smell the smoke when they were drilling in his bone.

"Now that's tough."

The late Boston Globe *sportswriter Will McDonough, a renowned tough guy himself—he once decked Pats cornerback Raymond Clayborn during a locker room confrontation—paid tribute when Grogan announced his retirement after the 1990 season. Grogan, McDonough wrote, was "a throwback who played the game for the game in an era of wimps who worry more about money than winning. … In brief, Steve Grogan has been what you hope every athlete turns out to be when they come into your community: an all-out performer who gives everything he has on and off the field over a long period of time."*

86

Kevin Millar
Red Sox First Baseman/Outfielder, 2003–2005

He didn't just talk the talk. He also walked the walk. And no walk ever meant more to the Boston Red Sox than the one Kevin Millar drew off of Yankees closer Mariano Rivera to lead off the last of the ninth in Game 4 of the 2004 ALCS, with the Sox trailing 3–0 in the series and 4–3 on Fenway's ancient scoreboard.

"Let me tell ya: Don't let us win today," Millar had told the *Boston Globe*'s Dan Shaughnessy earlier that evening. "Don't let the Sox win this game."

It would have been easy to dismiss Millar's remarks as empty bravado. Google any pregame story about any team that had ever faced a 3–0 deficit, and you'd be sure to find some dip-spittin' Pollyanna spouting a variation of Yogi Berra's "It ain't over till it's over."

But Millar's pronouncement was different. In hindsight it has an eerie prescience. What's striking is both the specificity of Millar's rationale and the authenticity in his defiance. "They got to win," Millar said, "because we got Pedey tomorrow and we got Schill in Game 6."

There was some sound baseball logic behind Millar's fightin' words. So far, the series hadn't conformed to form. In Game 1, a 10–7 Yankees win, Sox ace Curt Schilling had exited in the fourth inning with an ankle injury. In Game 2, journeyman Jon Lieber had outpitched two-time Cy Young Award winner Pedro Martinez. In Game 3, a 19–8 clown show, neither team's staff had distinguished itself. But if the Sox could just get through Game 4, they would have favorable pitching matchups in games 5 and 6.

If the Sox won those, all the pressure would be on the Yankees in Game 7. "We could put *you* out there," Millar told Shaughnessy. "Dan Shaughnessy, hitting ninth."

Shaughnessy had become the curly-hair-curtained face of New England's angst. His 1990 book *The Curse of the Bambino* distilled the frustration of all those slip-through-the-fingers seasons since 1918. If Sox players felt the weight of all the franchise's past failures, it was in large part because guys like Dan Shaughnessy constantly reminded them of it.

But this group seemed different—Millar in particular. He'd become a fan favorite in '03 because of his 25 homers, his "Cowboy up" catch phrase, and his "Rally Karaoke Guy" Springsteen video. A cool California native with some Texas seasoning, he provided an antidote to the agita.

And there he was telling Dan Shaughnessy to take his institutional pessimism and shove it. Millar didn't care that things looked hopeless—he liked the Sox' chances.

And now, in one of those cinematic moments that baseball specializes in, Millar had a chance to back up his brash talk. It was just past midnight when he stepped into the box against Rivera, with the Red Sox needing a run to live for another inning.

Don't let the Sox win this game.

Millar wasn't the only one who sensed what could happen. So did Rivera. "Nobody needs to remind us that this Red Sox team has a bunch of guys with pit-pull makeup, guys who are gamers," Rivera later wrote in his autobiography. He also noted that Millar "has had success against me."

Sure enough. Millar was hitting .364 off Rivera, with a home run.

Rivera fell behind in the count 3–1, with the lone strike a foul ball on a loud line drive.

Millar had gone to the plate thinking home run. He was in a great hitter's count. But he also trusted his teammates enough not to try to be a hero if the circumstances didn't present themselves.

Rivera's next pitch was up and in. Ball four.

In 67 prior postseason appearances, Rivera had walked the leadoff batter just twice—never while protecting a one-run lead. He hadn't issued any walks at all in his previous 16 postseason appearances.

Millar jogged to first. Then he passed the baton to pinch runner Dave Roberts, who stole the base that stole the game that stole the series and transformed Kevin Millar into a dirt-dog Nostradamus.

Do "clubhouse guys" like Kevin Millar really help win games? Pedro Martinez thought so. "Kevin Millar's free spirit infected us all," Pedro later asserted. And the results seemed to support that. The Red Sox made the playoffs in Millar's three seasons in Boston (2003–05)—but didn't in the seasons immediately before he arrived and after he left.

85

Kevin Faulk
Patriots Running Back/Returner, 1999–2011

S tats don't always tell the story. But in this case they provide a tidy synopsis. Kevin Faulk is among the New England Patriots' all-time top ten in rushing, receiving, punt returns, and kickoff returns. And he is the Pats' career leader in all-purpose yards, with 12,349.

Perfect. On a franchise that values versatility, Kevin Faulk was the consummate all-purpose Patriot.

Faulk, drafted in the second round out of LSU in 1999, was listed on the roster as a running back. But in his 13 seasons, all with the Patriots, he was rarely the featured back. (He led the team in rushing just once, in 2000.) Among those he deferred to were Antowain Smith, Corey Dillon, and Laurence Maroney. Even Sammy Watkins and BenJarvus Green-Ellis vaulted ahead of him on the depth chart.

Still, Faulk was a critical component on the offense—particularly as a third-down receiver. "He was a mismatch at all times," Tom Brady said, "and no one was more clutch than Kevin." Sixty-eight times during his career Faulk moved the chains with third-down catches. (He converted three fourth-down opportunities, too.)

Faulk also provided his share of electrifying returns, including a pair of kickoffs that he took to the house in 2002.

Faulk's value as a shape-shifting offensive weapon was never more evident than during a two-year stretch encompassing the 2002 and 2003 seasons. In '02, Faulk became the first Patriot to accomplish the three R's—touchdowns via rushing, receiving, and return—in the same season. A year later he didn't score at all until just 2:51 remained in the season, when he rushed for a crucial two-point conversion on a direct snap against the Carolina Panthers in Super Bowl XXXVIII.

"The bigger the situation," said coach Bill Belichick, "the more critical the play, the better he played and the more you could count on him."

Belichick also praised Faulk for his work ethic and team-first attitude. "In my coaching career, nobody has ever worked harder to do the things that he was asked to do," said Belichick. "Kevin was just so adept at figuring out his role, and doing it to the very best that he could. He was the ultimate team player."

Faulk enjoyed the ultimate reward for his team play. At his retirement announcement in 2012, he displayed the three Super Bowl rings he'd won with the Patriots. "I know I'm leaving the game of football," he said, "but I'm leaving with a little bit of jewelry."

84

Tim Thomas
Bruins Goalie, 2002–2012

He arrived quietly and departed amid a squall of sports-radio noise. In between, Tim Thomas gave Bruins fans two full seasons of Vezina Trophy goaltending—and the postseason of a lifetime. His play during the 2011 Stanley Cup Playoffs was one of the great money performances in Boston sports history. Thomas made a record 798 saves in the run to the Stanley Cup, including 238 in the Cup Final (another record). Three of the four series went seven games (the other was a sweep). Five of the 25 games went into sudden-death overtime. The Bruins won four of them.

After the lone OT loss, in Game 2 of the Cup Final against Vancouver, Thomas could have cracked. The winning goal came just 11 seconds into overtime, following a turnover. Thomas strayed too far from the net and Vancouver winger Alexandre Burrows scored on a wrap-around. This followed an equally devastating loss in the series opener, when Thomas surrendered the game's only goal with just 18 seconds left in regulation.

Down two games to none, the Bruins could have morphed into the '85 Patriots, an overachieving team that the Bears exposed in the Super Bowl. Thomas had already exceeded expectations just by carrying Boston to its first Cup Final in 21 years. Along the way the Bruins had bounced the hated Canadiens in round one (in OT of Game 7, no less). They had avenged an historic collapse from the previous year (when they had coughed up a 3–0 series lead) by sweeping the Flyers. And they had capped a seven-game stress fest in the Eastern Conference Final with a 1–0 win over the Lightning.

Really, what more could Boston have asked of its 37-year-old goaltender? The guy was such a long shot that he was 28 before he'd even made his first NHL start. Along the way he had meandered from Flint, Michigan, to the University of Vermont to Jokerit, Finland. At one point his parents sold their wedding rings to pay for his hockey camp in Ontario. He had finally earned a starting job at age 33—and then lost it at age 35. He regained it only after hip surgery.

Seriously, if the talented Canucks, who finished ten points ahead of the next-best team in the regular season, broomed the Bruins out of the Cup Final—well, Bruins fans would still have been indebted to their aging goalie just for carrying them as far as he did.

But Thomas wasn't thinking that way. He had located his emotional equilibrium long ago. "If you're in this business long enough," he'd said after his first NHL start, "you learn not to get surprised about too much and take everything as it goes."

Well, Thomas might not have been surprised by what happened next, but the rest of the hockey world was. Instead of crashing back to earth, Thomas elevated his game not only beyond anything he had ever achieved before, but also beyond what *any* goalie had ever achieved before. Over the final five games Thomas allowed just four goals. He set records for the fewest goals allowed in a seven-game final (8) and the highest save percentage (.967). He became the first goalie to record a shutout on the road in Game 7 of the Cup Final. And he became the oldest player to win the Conn Smythe Trophy as playoff MVP.

He was 37—two years younger than the Stanley Cup drought he had helped end in Boston.

The rest of Thomas's time in Boston was a contentious anticlimax. A staunch political conservative, Thomas declined to join the rest of the Bruins when they visited the Barack Obama White House the following January. Three months later Washington got its revenge, as the Capitals bounced Thomas and the Bruins from the Stanley Cup Playoffs in the first round. After that Thomas announced that he was taking a "sabbatical" from hockey. He never played for the Bruins again.

83

Satch Sanders
Celtics Forward, 1960–1973

In 13 seasons as a power forward, all with the Celtics, Tom "Satch" Sanders had exactly one 30-point game—and he scored exactly 30 points in that one. But he won eight NBA championships. Only Bill Russell and Sam Jones have won more

The guy got his money's worth. That was obvious from the way he played defense. Sanders was allotted six personal fouls per game, and he often used them all. When the Celtics beat the Lakers in the 1963 NBA Finals, Sanders committed 32 fouls in six games. In 1965 he fouled out 11 times in the Celtics' first 16 games. (Larry Bird fouled out just 11 times in his career.) With 94 foul-outs, Sanders is the franchise leader.

His philosophy was simple: No freebies.

Sanders, who had set several scoring records at NYU, was the Celtics' first-round draft pick in 1960. But Red Auerbach, Bull Russell & Co. made it clear that if he wanted to be a part of their long-term plans, he'd better bring his hard hat. Asked before the season what he saw in Sanders, Auerbach said, "First of all, his defensive ability. He is a hungry ballplayer, one who wants to make good, who wants to win. He has long arms and can clear the boards. And mainly, he has desire."

The Celtics brought Sanders along slowly during his rookie season, using him mainly to spell Tom Heinsohn and Frank Ramsey. It wasn't until the playoffs, when the Celtics faced the Syracuse Nationals in the Eastern Division Finals, that Auerbach used Sanders to full effect. With the series even at one game each, Red made Sanders a surprise starter in Game 3. Sanders responded with 13 points and nine rebounds in just 19 minutes. He then went for a double-double in each of the two remaining games as the Celtics closed out the Nats in five.

But Sanders's biggest contribution was the suffocating defense he applied against Dolph Schayes, Syracuse's leading scorer. Schayes averaged 29 points per game over the first two games of the Eastern Division Finals—but just 19.3 points per game over the final three, when Sanders focused on stopping him.

It was the first real glimpse of what Sanders would unleash on Celtics' opponents for the next decade. And it was now clear why Auerbach had made him a No. 1 pick. "How'd he get away from us in the draft?" Schayes lamented after the series. "We should have grabbed him. He would have made us."

Said Red, "I want to say this about Tom Sanders: He is a tremendously hard worker. He was always willing to sacrifice in order to do the job we wanted from him."

And then Auerbach summed up why Satch Sanders was such a good fit in Boston: "Let's just say he has the 'Celtics' attitude."

Sanders maintained his Celtics attitude for the rest of his career. When Bill Russell and Sam Jones retired in 1969, it was Sanders who mentored rookie Jo Jo White. White later joked that during cross-country flights, "We'd say, 'Don't sit next to Satch,' because he'd talk to you all the way from Boston to LA." After retiring as a player Sanders coached at Harvard for four years before serving briefly as the Celtics' coach over parts of two seasons. He was an associate director at the Center for the Study of Sport in Society at Northeastern, and he founded the NBA's Rookie Transition Program. In 2011 he was inducted into the Naismith Memorial Basketball Hall of Fame as a "contributor," a fitting description of the role he played on those eight title-winning Celtics teams.

82

Bruce Armstrong
Patriots Tackle, 1987–2000

How could an 0–7 start get any worse? The 1992 Patriots got their answer in Game 8 at Buffalo, when Bills defensive end Bruce Smith fell on Bruce Armstrong's right leg. The Patriots' Pro Bowl left tackle's knee buckled. A streak of 84 starts that extended to his rookie season (1987) came to an agonizing end.

The injury looked serious. And it was. Armstrong had torn not only his MCL and his ACL, but also his PCL (posterior cruciate ligament). A Pats press release, providing far more detail in that pre-Belichick era, declared that the injury would require "at least a year of rehabilitation," and that "the extent of the injury could impair Armstrong's ability to play football again."

Scroll ahead ten months, and go back to Buffalo. An 0–1 start had never looked better. Sure, the Patriots got smoked, 38–14. But they had a new coach (Bill Parcells), a new quarterback (Drew Bledsoe), and a new outlook.

They also had their old left tackle back. Bruce Armstrong, defying all expectations, started the 1993 season opener. "I never doubted myself as much as others doubted my ability to be back this early," he said. "This game was always what I was working toward."

Armstrong played eight more seasons and never missed another game—despite playing most of the 1995 season with a torn anterior capsule in his right shoulder and undergoing another knee surgery before his fourteenth and final season in 2000.

Armstrong, who made the Pro Bowl six times, is the only Patriot to have played under Raymond Berry, Bill Parcells, and Bill Belichick.

Of playing under Parcells, a notorious taskmaster, he said, "When you have a coach who's not always easy to get along with, you have to be the filter between the coach and the kids so they understand exactly what he means, so we're all pulling in the same direction. ... It's things like showing up on time for meetings and wearing the proper equipment. You have to explain that it's important to earn the respect of your teammates."

Armstrong earned enough respect from Parcells to be named a team captain. Noting that Armstrong's iron-man streak extended beyond game days, Parcells said, "He never misses a practice, and I mean never."

Under Parcells, Armstrong played in Super Bowl XXXI, which he called "the pot of gold you've always heard about."

Armstrong officially announced his retirement in September 2001—coincidentally the same week that the Jets' Mo Lewis ended Drew Bledsoe's run as the Patriots starter. Armstrong, who had guarded Bledsoe's blind side for eight seasons, still felt protective of his QB. Said Armstrong, "I would have been the first one to tell him, next time get his ass out of bounds."

Pats owner Robert Kraft dispensed with the customary five-year waiting period and inducted Armstrong into the Patriots Hall of Fame immediately upon his retirement. This inadvertently created a nice bit of symmetry. The Patriots retired Armstrong's number, 78, at halftime of the Pats–Colts game at Gillette Stadium on September 30, 2001. That was also the first career start for Tom Brady—who in 2015 passed Armstrong on the list for most games played in Patriots history.

81

Derek Sanderson
Bruins Center, 1965–1972; 1973–1974

He was a charter member of the Big Bad Bruins. Derek Sanderson was a wily center with a left-handed shot and a swashbuckler's sense of style. With his long hair and sideburns, he looked like he'd wandered away from Woodstock. But he had the same old-school grit as Eddie Shore.

Take that night at the Garden in November 1970, when the Bruins and Canadiens staged one of their nastiest brawls ever. Sanderson was the third man in on a fight between Wayne Cashman and Canadiens defenseman Guy Lapointe. That put a match to the powder keg. Gloves and sticks littered the rink as every player on each team looked for someone to square off with. Sanderson ended up tussling with Montreal winger Phil Roberto right in front of the Habs' bench. Then Canadiens' coach Claude Ruel got involved.

Mistake. Sanderson vaulted over the boards into the enemy bench area. Ruel was lucky that there were a couple of Boston cops there to restrain Sanderson.

The sold-out Garden crowd loved it. This was Derek Sanderson before all the wretched 1970s excesses that would eventually derail his career. It wasn't his fashion sense that helped the Bruins win two Stanley Cups in three years. Nor his fighting skills—or at least not his fighting skills alone. Mostly, it was all the little battles he won during the flow of the game. Like face-offs. Or penalty kills.

Another telltale indicator of Sanderson's effectiveness: shorthanded goals. He had 24 for the Bruins. Only Rick Middleton, with 25, had more—and he played more than twice as many games as Sanderson did. Sanderson added six more shorthanded goals in postseason play, including three in one year.

Sanderson also had a good rapport with Bobby Orr. They came up a year apart; Orr received the Calder Trophy as the NHL's rookie of the year in 1967; Sanderson followed suit in 1968. Their best display of chemistry happened on May 10, 1970, 40 seconds into sudden death overtime of Game 4 of the Stanley Cup Final against St. Louis.

Everyone remembers the photo of that moment: The Flying Orr goal. But not everyone remembers that it was Derek Sanderson who set it up with a perfect pass from behind the net. Said Sanderson, "I made the kid famous."

In 2011, GQ magazine named its "25 Coolest Athletes of All Time." Two played for Boston teams (not counting Pistol Pete Maravich, who played 26 games with the Celtics.) One was Tom Brady. The other was Derek Sanderson.

80

Tony Conigliaro
Red Sox Outfielder, 1964–1967; 1968–1970; 1975

He was a local kid, and that always counts for a lot in New England. Tony Conigliaro—born in Revere, signed out of St. Mary's High in Lynn at age 17, and playing for the Red Sox by age 19. First time up at Fenway he hit a first-pitch fastball completely out of the park. He celebrated with a huge Italian dinner at his parents' house in Swampscott.

Conigliaro added 23 more home runs in that '64 season, the most ever hit by any major leaguer before age 20.

It was good that Bostonians had a local boy to cheer for in the mid-60s because the team offered little else to get excited about. The 1965 Red Sox lost 100 games. But Conigliaro played spirited defense in right and led the American League with 32 homers. He also added a handful of memorable singles—in the recording studio. (Check out the Beach Boys-esque "Little Red Scooter" on YouTube.) And he dated a supermodel or two. Had he played for the Red Sox today, Tony C. would have achieved a Gronk-like level of popularity.

He was well on his way to that status in August 1967. He was having another solid season, with 20 homers and a .287 average—and this time he had help. The Red Sox were in a pennant race, and Fenway was banged out on a regular basis for the first time in years. The Sox were just 3½ games back on Friday, August 18, when the Angels arrived for a four-game series.

It was still 0–0 in the bottom of the fourth. Two outs and no one on. Conigliaro up. A fastball from Angels righthander Jack Hamilton sailed up and in. Conigliaro couldn't react quickly enough. The ball hit him in the left eye, fracturing his orbital bone, dislocating his cheek, and causing swelling in his retina.

The crowd of 31,027 fell silent. Tony C's teammates carried him off the field on a stretcher.

Conigliaro missed not just the rest of the Impossible Dream season, but all of the next season as well. In the spring of '68, doctors at the Massachusetts Eye & Ear Infirmary and the Retina Foundation offered a grim prognosis. Scar tissue behind his left retina had affected Conigliaro's depth perception. It seemed highly unlikely that he would ever face another major league fastball.

But on Opening Day 1969, Conigliaro made his return in Baltimore. And what a return: After a 20-month absence, Tony C. shook off the rust and any lingering trauma from that Fenway beaning to blast a two-run homer in the tenth inning, helping the Red Sox to a 5–4 win over the Orioles.

Tony's father, Sal, watched the game from work, at the Triangle Tool and Dye Co. in Lynn. "The day he walked out of that Retina Foundation a year ago, we never thought he could make a move on the field again," Sal said. "It's another remarkable step in his life. Only this is the most remarkable step of them all."

Despite that triumphal return, neither Tony Conigliaro's career nor his life ended well. He hit a respectable 20 home runs in 1969, and followed up with career highs in home runs (36) and RBI (116) in 1970. And then the Red Sox traded him to the Angels. Conigliaro appeared in just 74 games with his new team before ending his career with a sad 21-game swan song back in Boston in 1975. Seven years later he suffered a heart attack. He died of kidney failure in 1990, at just 45 years old.

79

Logan Mankins
Patriots Left Guard, 2005–2013

Bill Belichick called him "one of the all-time great Patriots and the best guard I ever coached." Logan Mankins was also one of the toughest Patriots ever; he played the entire 2011 season with a torn ACL. Then he brushed that accomplishment aside. "It wasn't 100%" he said of his injured knee, "but it was still functional. ... Put a brace on, tape an aspirin to it, and go. If I can run, I'm not going to sit out any game. I'm here to play football, not to watch and collect a check."

Mankins displayed that same offhand dedication from the time he arrived as a first-round pick from Fresno State in 2005. Replacing the starting left guard on the two-time, defending Super Bowl champions would have been daunting enough. (Joe Andruzzi, a five-year Pats veteran, had departed via free agency.) Adding to the challenge, Mankins hadn't even played that position in college—he'd been a left tackle.

Mankins rose to the task. "He's a workhorse," center Dan Koppen said during training camp. "He keeps his mouth shut and does what he's told to do."

"He's a hillbilly," veteran linebacker Mike Vrabel said of Mankins, who had driven to Foxboro from rural California in a 1987 Ford pickup with 200,000 miles on it. "I think he's going to be a good fit for us."

Vrabel was right. Mankins not only started every game in his first season, but he also played well enough at guard to make *Pro Football Weekly*'s All-Rookie team. He didn't miss a start in his first five seasons in New England, and by his third year he was named to the Pro Bowl. It was the first of his six Pro Bowl selections as a Patriot.

It's unfortunate—and unfair—that Mankins's time in New England is notable more for what didn't happen than what did. His Pats career coincided with the nine-year drought between title No. 3 and title No. 4. Although Mankins was still playing at a high level in 2014, his age (32) and salary ($6.25 million) made him vulnerable to the Pats' unforgiving actuarial table. He was dealt to the Tampa Bay Buccaneers for tight end Tim Wright and a fourth-round draft pick.

It had to be a bitter blow. But if ever a player was constitutionally suited to handle the harsh reality of pro football, it was Logan Mankins. "If you don't understand that it's a business, you're lying to yourself," he said. "You have to be prepared for whatever happens in this league at any time."

He added: "I have nothing bad to say about New England. I love that place."

The feeling was mutual.

Mankins's true value became apparent in 2015, long after he was gone. The Patriots' offensive line was shaky all season, and finally imploded in a brutal 20–18 loss at Denver in the AFC Championship Game. Meanwhile, Mankins quietly made his seventh Pro Bowl that year, with the Bucs.

78

Tiny Thompson
Bruins Goalie, 1928–1938

He arrived in 1928, the same year Boston Garden opened. And even if he had never played another season in the NHL, Bruins goalie Tiny Thompson would have assured his place in Boston sports history based on his rookie year alone. In his first start, at Pittsburgh, Thompson—who came to the Bruins from the AHL's Minneapolis Millers by way of Calgary—beat the Pirates 1–0 in overtime. That set the standard. It was the first of Thompson's 12 shutouts that season, and his 1.15 goals-against average still stands as the best in Bruins history—and the fourth-best in NHL history.

But it would have been for naught if the Bruins, a fifth-year franchise, hadn't won their first Stanley Cup that season. En route to winning the Cup, the Bruins upset the NHL's best team, the Montreal Canadiens—or "Flying Frenchmen" as the Boston press invariably called them—in a first-round sweep. Thompson was magnificent, allowing just two goals in three games. A boisterous crowd descended on North Station to greet the Bruins' train when it returned from Montreal after the decisive third game. Clearly, hockey had gained a toehold as a major professional sport in Boston. "Heretofore," John J. Hallahan wrote in the *Boston Globe*, "only the Olympic athletes of 1896 and World Series baseball champions have been accorded such a tribute."

Much of that adoration was directed at Boston's rookie goalie, "who saved the Bruins at the Garden last Thursday," Hallahan wrote, "and gave one of the greatest exhibitions of stopping flying rubber ever seen on Saturday night. … They will tell you in Montreal that Thompson alone beat the Canadiens."

Although Thompson never won another Stanley Cup, he remained a popular and influential goalie who was inducted into the Hockey Hall of Fame in 1959. He used a "stand-up" style, which wasn't easy considering his height. (The nickname "Tiny," as is usually the case, was used ironically; at 5'10" Thompson was actually tall for his time.) He was one of the first goalies to catch the puck instead of deflecting it. He was also the first goalie pulled for an extra skater (in the 1931 Stanley Cup Playoffs) and the first goalie to record an assist. He was a four-time Vezina Trophy winner and is still the Bruins' all-time leader in minutes (28,948), wins (252), shutouts (74), and GAA (1.99). He died in 1981.

77

Johnny Pesky
Red Sox Infielder, 1942; 1946–1952

To later generations of Sox fans, he was an avuncular figure who was simply *there*. You'd see him at every Red Sox game, every spring training, every team function—the kind of guy invariably dubbed "the mayor" at small towns all over New England. He was an ever-present link to the team's star-crossed, black-and-white past.

But his former teammates saw something else. In their minds, Johnny Pesky was forever young and vital—a burst of color on the base paths and at shortstop. Said Ted Williams, "It didn't take an expert to see he was going to make it real big right from the start with that quick bat, blazing speed, and good glove."

Pesky put himself in rarefied company from the outset. He topped 200 hits in each of his first three seasons, becoming just the sixth major leaguer to have done so to that point. But there was an asterisk attached to Pesky's accomplishment. It took him six years to play those three seasons, because he served as a navy aviator during World War II. He had begun his training at Amherst College even before his rookie year ended.

The obvious question is, What did those three years cost Pesky? But a better question is, What did those three years cost the Red Sox? Every major league team lost players to WWII service, but the Sox felt the loss more acutely than most. In 1942, Williams and Pesky finished second and third in MVP voting, respectively. The Sox lost the services of both, along with centerfielder Dom DiMaggio and right-handed pitcher Charlie Wagner, for the next three years. In addition, future Hall of Fame second baseman Bobby Doerr missed the 1945 season. In

1946 the reunited Red Sox responded by posting Boston's only 100-win season (104–50) between 1915 and 2018.

That season ended in bitter disappointment, however, when the Sox dropped Game 7 of the World Series to the Cardinals, 4–3. Cards rightfielder Enos Slaughter scored the deciding run in the bottom of the eighth, coming around all the way from first on what looked at the crack of the bat to be a routine single to center. Slaughter, who was running on the pitch, attempted to score only because DiMaggio, who had a terrific arm, had left the game with an injury. Slaughter easily beat the throw from DiMaggio's backup, Leon Culberson, to Pesky, who relayed it home.

It was heads-up baserunning. Nothing more. But in the aftermath, based on the real-time, naked-eye judgment of a wire-service reporter —there was no live TV coverage, let alone instant replay—Pesky became a scapegoat. Allegedly, he held the ball on the relay. A surviving film debunks this, but the allegation stuck.

Pesky took the finger-pointing in stride. "If you're a palooka," he said years later, "you've got to live with it."

Adding to that perceived palooka-dom in later years was "Pesky's Pole" at Fenway. Sox pitcher Mel Parnell, who became a broadcaster in the 1960s, coined the term, ribbing his old teammate for his lack of power. Pesky had just 17 career home runs, with only six coming at Fenway. Parnell noted that Pesky needed the short right-field foul line (302 feet) just to hit those.

Pesky's Pole now stands as a mixed blessing. Yes, it immortalizes the name Johnny Pesky. But it emphasizes his shortcomings rather than the impressive package of talent who led the American League in hits for three years running, right out of the gate. As his first manager, Joe Cronin, once said, "He was phenomenal in those first three seasons. You couldn't ask for more than he gave."

Pesky, who died in 2012, continued to give to the Red Sox in many ways. Besides his eight years as a player, Pesky provided the Red Sox another 53 years of service as a manager, a broadcaster, a third-base coach, a special instructor, a spokesman, and a goodwill ambassador. The Red Sox retired his number (6) in 2008.

76

Corey Dillon
Patriots Running Back, 2004–2006

Under Bill Belichick the Patriots have let a lot of productive running backs walk. Think BenJarvus Green-Ellis (1,008 yards, 13 touchdowns in 2010). Or Stevan Ridley (1,263 yards and 12 touchdowns in 2012). Or Jonas Gray (201 yards and four touchdowns in one *game* in 2014). In New England, a prospective back's most valuable skill is the ability to run through a revolving door.

All of which makes Corey Dillon's tenure even more impressive.

The Patriots had ridden Dillon's predecessor, Antowain Smith, to two Super Bowl wins in three seasons. But the Pats declined to pick up Smith's option, then traded a second-round pick for Dillon on the eve of the 2004 NFL draft. Pats brass thought that Dillon, who was faster than Smith and almost as big, would be the ideal backfield complement for Tom Brady.

Still, the trade generated some anxiety in New England. As a Cincinnati Bengal, Dillon had a reputation as an outspoken malcontent who had once walked off the field during a game. But in his defense: Who *wouldn't* have been tempted to walk out on those dreadful Bengals teams? As good as Dillon was—in seven seasons in Cincinnati he amassed more than 8,000 yards rushing and scored 50 touchdowns—he couldn't carry the load all by himself.

The Patriots offered Dillon a fresh start and the chance to play on a winner for the first time. "I didn't come here to rot away and take Ls," he said. "I want to be part of something that is a winning tradition and this is it."

Dillon played a major role in continuing that winning tradition. In 2004 he set a franchise record with 1,635 yards rushing on 345 carries as the Pats repeated as Super Bowl champions. Nine times that year he ran for more than 100 yards in a game. The Patriots were 14–1 with him in the lineup. In the lone game he missed (because of a thigh injury), at Pittsburgh on Halloween, the Patriots gained just five yards rushing in six attempts and had their record 21-game winning streak snapped.

In his first postseason start, against the Colts in a division-round game at Gillette Stadium, Dillon gained 144 yards on 23 carries. He was also the Pats' leading receiver, catching all five passes that Brady threw him. The game plan, which called for keeping Indianapolis quarterback Peyton Manning off the field, worked to perfection. The Patriots dominated in both time of possession (37:43 to 22:17) and on the scoreboard (20–3). And their workhorse back earned a new nickname: "Clock-Killin' Corey Dillon."

Dillon also played a major role in a rematch with the Steelers at Pittsburgh in the AFC Championship Game. He had a 25-yard touchdown run in the third quarter to give the Pats a 21-point lead, and his nine fourth-quarter carries helped salt the game away.

Dillon capped his stellar first season in New England with 75 yards and a touchdown on 18 carries in the Super Bowl against Philadelphia. He added three catches for 31 yards, including a pair of critical second-quarter screen passes that helped neutralize the Eagles' blitz-happy defense.

In his first try with the Pats, Dillon had reached his career-long goal. Along the way he had also earned the admiration of his new teammates. Said Tom Brady, "He's the best running back in the league."

Dillon played just two more seasons in New England. And although he continued to produce—he had a career-high 13 rushing touchdowns his final season—he decided to walk away while he still could. "I don't want to be broken down, not able to play with my kids," he said. His only regret was that he couldn't have come to New England sooner. "I look at the whole last three years and they were the best three years of my career," he said. "It was all that a guy could ask for. When I look back, that group helped me get where I needed to go."

75

Cedric Maxwell
Celtics Forward, 1977–1985

W ould you rather be a star on a terrible team or one of many contributors on a winner? For Cedric Maxwell that wasn't a hypothetical question. His answer was clear. "What I'm really proud of is that I wasn't a selfish player," Maxwell said in 2003, when the Celtics retired his jersey number, 31, to the Garden rafters. "I sacrificed my personal numbers for the team. Before Larry was here, I was almost a 20-10 guy. My numbers went down because I looked at it as an opportunity to win."

Those numbers spoke for themselves. Maxwell arrived in Boston in the fall of '77, the start of one of the most dysfunctional stretches in franchise history. In his first two seasons Maxwell had three coaches and zero playoff appearances. He also had career highs in points per game (19.0) and rebounds per game (9.9).

Then Larry Bird arrived. The Celtics won as many games in Bird's rookie season (61) as they had in the previous two seasons combined. Maxwell's scoring dipped, but another number was more telling. He shot 60.9% from the field, still a Celtics record. That showed how he relished being a complementary player on a winning team.

But the real change came in 1980, when Robert Parish and Kevin McHale arrived. The original incarnation of the Big Three was complete. Maxwell became what he called "the fourth Musketeer." And he was fine with that. "He couldn't have been more supportive," said McHale, who usurped much of Maxwell's playing time.

Hubie Brown, who faced the nightmare of matching up against those Celtics teams as an opposing coach, recognized what Maxwell brought to the parquet. "He fit perfectly within the group," said Brown. "He could score, he could defend, he could rebound."

Among other things, Maxwell often took the most challenging defensive assignment, freeing Bird to concentrate on his offense. "The fact that he guarded all the tough guys really helped my career," said Bird.

And it wasn't as if Maxwell *always* played a subordinate role. In fact, when the Celtics won a championship in the Big Three's first season together, Maxwell was the team's leading scorer in the Finals against Houston. He was named MVP. And when the Celtics won another title in 1984, against the Lakers, Maxwell made the difference in a tense Game 7 at the Garden. He led the team in points (24), assists (eight), and minutes (43), and added eight rebounds, two steals, a blocked shot, and merciless verbal harassment of Lakers forward James Worthy. "I just told him he couldn't guard me," Maxwell said afterward.

He didn't restrict his boasts to the opposition, either. Before the game he delivered a message to his Celtics teammates: "I said, 'Well, boys, one more time. Just hop on my back.' I've always been a big-game player, and tonight was a big game."

On a team of notorious trash talkers, Maxwell might have been the trashiest talker of all. It was just part of the Celtics' calculated swagger. "I would say in 25% of the Celtics' wins, we beat a team mentally before they stepped on the floor," Maxwell said.

That Game 7 win over LA was his finest hour. Afterward, he gave a shout-out to the Celtics' *real* Big Three. Said Cedric Maxwell, "We have character, courage, and poise."

Even when he left town, Cedric Maxwell unwittingly contributed to a Celtics title. Unhappy with Maxwell's effort to rehab from a knee injury, Red Auerbach dealt Maxwell to the LA Clippers for Bill Walton in 1985. Walton, of course, became the sixth man on one of the greatest teams in NBA history. Mutual resentment between Maxwell and the Celtics lingered for a decade. It ended in 1995 when Maxwell became an analyst on Celtics radio broadcasts, a role he still has.

74

Drew Bledsoe
Patriots Quarterback, 1993–2001

People forget. Before he lost his starting job (and almost lost his life), Drew Bledsoe helped save the New England Patriots. When he arrived in 1993, as a No. 1 pick from Washington State, Bledsoe joined a team that had finished 2–14 the year before. Home attendance averaged just 38,551 a game. Spurred by the addition of Bledsoe (along with head coach Bill Parcells), season ticket sales spiked. By 1995 they were well north of 50,000.

During that interim, season-ticket holder Robert Kraft bought the team, ending months of speculation that the previous owner, James Orthwein, intended to move the Patriots to St. Louis.

On the field, Bledsoe helped engineer several comebacks that were almost as dramatic. On November 13, 1994, the 3–6 Patriots trailed the 7–2 Vikings 20–0 at Foxboro. By day's end the Patriots had won 26–20 and Bledsoe had set a pair of NFL records that still stand: most pass attempts in a game (70) and most completions (45).

Then there was the last game of the '96 season, when the Pats trailed the Giants 22–0 at halftime. Bledsoe had been awful, throwing a pick-six and committing intentional grounding in the end zone for a safety. But he bounced back with a couple of second-half touchdown passes to give the Pats a 23–22 win and a first-round bye in the playoffs. New England ended up making the Super Bowl for just the second time in 37 seasons.

Bledsoe was also on the field five years later when the Patriots beat the Steelers 24–17 in the AFC Championship Game. He entered in the last two minutes of the first half after Tom Brady rolled his ankle. It was the first game action Bledsoe had seen in four months, since he had lost his starting job—first to injury, then to a coach's decision.

Bledsoe completed his first three passes, finishing a touchdown drive that put the Pats up 14–3 at the half, en route to another Super Bowl.

Brady, of course, returned as the starter for that Super Bowl, against the St. Louis Rams. Bledsoe returned to the bench.

His life had changed dramatically with a single play on September 23, 2001. People remember the moment. (Some Pats fans, perversely, even celebrate it.) Jets linebacker Mo Lewis drilled Bledsoe on a third-down scramble along the sideline, short of the first-down marker.

But people forget the details. They forget, for instance, that the Lewis hit didn't knock Bledsoe out of the game—at least not immediately. Before yielding to Tom Brady, Bledsoe returned to the field for the next series. The Pats trailed 10–3 with 3½ minutes left. On third-and-seven, with the ball on the Jets 36, Bledsoe hit fullback Marc Edwards for a two-yard gain, but Edwards fumbled the ball away.

All Pats fans ought to pause and acknowledge that moment. On his final play as the New England Patriots' starting quarterback, Drew Bledsoe completed a pass. He did so despite having a concussion, and a chest that was filling with blood from a sheared artery—an injury severe enough to land him in the ICU at Mass General after the game.

That's another thing people tend to forget about Bledsoe: his toughness. In his last two full seasons as the starter, he was sacked an even 100 times, yet didn't miss a game.

When he finally lost his starting job, it was due to a life-threatening injury. And the guy who replaced him turned out to be the best quarterback in NFL history.

There's no shame in that.

Less than three months after Super Bowl XXXVIII, the Patriots traded Drew Bledsoe to the Bills for a first-round draft pick. He played three seasons in Buffalo and two in Dallas before retiring in 2007. On September 17, 2011—just before the tenth anniversary of the Mo Lewis hit—Bledsoe was inducted into the Patriots Hall of Fame.

73

Mookie Betts
Red Sox Outfielder, 2014–

Baseball, more so than any other sport, judges players by a double standard. The 162-game regular season gives great players time to show what separates them from average players. But the postseason, with its tiny sample size, can turn an average player into a star (hello, Steve Pearce) and a great player into a bust.

That's why Mookie Betts's 2018 season was so rewarding. He followed up an MVP-worthy regular season with a World Series title. And while his postseason performance was less flashy, Betts still demonstrated his full range of skills on baseball's biggest stage.

Red Sox fans already knew how versatile Mookie was. With his combination of speed, power, and an ability to put the ball in play, Betts can excel hitting either leadoff or cleanup. In 2016, when he finished second to Mike Trout in AL MVP voting, Betts did both (he hit first in 109 games and fourth in 36 games). But his numbers had an odd dissonance. He hit for a higher average and drew a higher percentage of walks as a cleanup hitter while producing much better power numbers out of the leadoff spot.

Once he was installed as the full-time leadoff hitter under new manager Alex Cora in 2018, Betts achieved a scary new level of consistency. He reached career highs in batting average (a league-best .346, which was an 82-point improvement over 2017), walks (81), and stolen bases (30)—all traditional benchmarks for a table-setter. But just as impressive, he surrendered none of his power. His 32 home runs were a career high, and his .640 slugging percentage topped his previous best by more than 100 points.

Yes, his RBI dipped, from 113 in 2016 to just 80 in 2018. But that was to be expected from a leadoff hitter on a team with a weak lower third of the batting order. The more telling stat was runs scored. Betts led the league with 129 (a career high), in just 136 games.

If there was one at-bat that typified Mookie Betts in 2018, it was his epic 13-pitch showdown with Toronto Blue Jays lefthander J.A. Happ on July 12. After falling behind 1–2, Betts battled back to a full count—fouling off six straight pitches at one point—before launching a game-changing grand slam deep into the summer night.

And in 2018 Betts's clutch play continued long after summer's warmth had yielded to an October chill. His first two postseason appearances, in 2016 and 2017, had lasted only through the first round. In 2018, with the Sox powering to a World Series title, Betts showed America what a complete player he is. Although he hit just .205 with no home runs through the ALDS and ALCS, he still played a key role. In the five-game Championship Series win over the Astros, Betts led the Red Sox with five runs scored, including first-inning runs in three straight games that put the pressure on Houston pitchers. Boston won all three games to take a 3–1 series lead.

Betts also contributed two highlight-reel defensive plays in Game 4 that helped turn a potential loss into a series-tilting win. In the first inning he leaped above the rightfield fence to try to snag a drive from Jose Altuve, which resulted in a fan-interference call that negated a two-run homer. In the eighth he threw out Tony Kemp with a guided missile to second that dampened an Astros comeback attempt.

By dispatching a pair of 100-win teams with relative ease to reach the World Series against the Dodgers, the Red Sox proved that their 108-win regular season was no mirage—and neither were Mookie's MVP numbers.

Yes, Betts's offense in the World Series fell far short of his regular-season production—including a conspicuous 0-for-7 in an 18-inning loss in Game 3. But he was the only Sox player with a three-hit game (a Game 2 win at Fenway). And his first postseason home run, off Clayton Kershaw in the Game 5 clincher, doubled the Sox lead from one run to two in the sixth inning and started the countdown toward Boston's fourth World Series title of the century.

72

Willie McGinest
Patriots Linebacker, Defensive End, 1994–2005

Like the other 73,000 or so astonished onlookers at the Louisiana Superdome, Patriots linebacker Willie McGinest was transfixed as Tebucky Jones sprinted 97 yards to the opposite end zone. With just over ten minutes remaining in Super Bowl XXXVI, Jones had scooped up a Kurt Warner fumble and returned it for an apparent touchdown and a devastating 14-point swing. Even "The Greatest Show on Turf," the St. Louis Rams, would have had trouble overcoming a 24–3 deficit that late in the game.

"I never saw the flag," McGinest said later.

After the play the officials huddled. The call: *Holding, defense, No. 55 …*

It was yet another dizzying swing in a season marked by extreme emotional fluctuations. The September 11 attacks. The loss of starting quarterback Drew Bledsoe. The surprising emergence of Bledsoe's backup, Tom Brady. An even more surprising run to the playoffs. And most surprising of all, a reprieve in the divisional round thanks to the Tuck Rule, when the game against Oakland appeared lost.

Through it all, McGinest had struggled to come back from offseason back surgery. He'd made just five starts, fewest of his 12-year Pats career. But he'd played well against Pittsburgh in the AFC Championship Game, registering a sack and two other tackles for losses. And against the Rams he was a key part of the Patriots' defensive game plan, which called for mugging running back Marshall Faulk on every play, whether he had the ball or not.

That's what McGinest did on the play when Warner fumbled. But he got called for it. The Rams cashed in two plays later to make it 17–10, then tied the game with just 1:37 left.

As of that date—February 3, 2002—the Patriots had yet to win a Super Bowl. No Boston team had won a title in more than 15 years, a period marked by some brutal collapses. If the Pats had let this one get away, Willie McGinest would have achieved instant induction into the Boston Sports Hall of Infamy.

But McGinest never let such thoughts enter his mind. Instead, he said, "I was thinking we'd find a way to win it."

They did, of course, when their unflappable young QB led the team on a 53-yard drive to set up Adam Vinatieri's 48-yard field goal. But the Patriots defense deserved its due in that monumental upset, too. And Willie McGinest was a vital component of that defense—just as he was on the defenses that won back-to-back Super Bowls in 2003 and 2004.

So it's fair and just that McGinest was spared eternal goatdom. Instead Pats fans remember him as the guy who put up two Pro Bowl seasons seven years apart, in 1996 and 2003. They remember him as the NFL's leader in post-season sacks in one game (4.5 vs. Jacksonville in 2006) and all-time (16.0). They remember the time he outwitted Peyton Manning, pretending he would drop into coverage and then stuffing Edgerrin James on fourth-and-goal from the one with 11 seconds left, preserving a 38–34 win at Indy. Or his pick-six against Jim Kelly in the final minute of a 28–25 win at Buffalo. Or any of the hundreds of other intelligent plays Willie McGinest made as he ground through every minute of every game thinking the Patriots would find a way to win.

After the Patriots released him in a salary cap maneuver in 2006, McGinest played three seasons in Cleveland before retiring. He was inducted into the Patriots Hall of Fame in 2015. Said Pats chairman and CEO Robert Kraft, "Just a few months after I bought the Patriots, we drafted Willie McGinest in the first round of the 1994 NFL Draft. We came into the NFL together and will always share a special bond. During his 12-year Patriots career, Willie played a critical role in transforming us from a cellar dweller into a championship-caliber team."

71

Bill Sharman
Celtics Guard, 1951–1961

How's this for delivering in the clutch? In 1959 Bill Sharman made 56 consecutive free throws in the NBA playoffs. It's a record that still stands.

Sharman, who never shot less than 84% from the line during his ten Celtics seasons, actually got better with age. His reached his career high, 92%, in his last year, when he was 34—ancient by 1961 standards.

Sharman continued to improve for a simple reason: He worked at it. Halfway through his career he found that if he practiced his shooting the morning of a game, he shot better that night. (Later, when he became a coach, Sharman implemented the "morning shoot-around," now an NBA staple.)

He was the rare athlete who was as competitive as he was talented. His backcourt mate, Bob Cousy, called him "the best athlete I've ever played with or against." Once, in a single day at his California high school, Sharman starred at a track meet in the morning (winning the shot put and discuss events); won a tennis tournament in the afternoon; and was the winning pitcher for his baseball team that evening. In 1950, he was drafted out of USC by both the Brooklyn Dodgers and the NBA's Washington Capitols. When the Capitols folded in January 1951, halfway through his rookie season, Sharman simply switched his attention to baseball. He was in the Dodgers' dugout that October when the Giants' Bobby Thomson hit his famed "shot heard 'round the world."

Sharman had planned to play winter ball in Cuba that year. But Red Auerbach (who had acquired Sharman's NBA rights in a typical

Auerbachian heist) persuaded him to give pro basketball another shot.

It ended up being a perfect marriage. Sharman spent his entire Celtics career paired with Cousy. They created the template for the modern NBA backcourt, matching a prototypical point guard with a pure shooting guard. Together, Cousy and Sharman turned the Celtics (a team that had finished a collective 39 games under .500 during its first five seasons) into a playoff perennial.

As great as they were, Boston's backcourt tandem could carry the team only so far. In each of Sharman's first five seasons, the Celtics failed to win the Eastern Division. When Bill Russell and Tom Heinsohn arrived in the fall of '56, Boston had a frontcourt that was the equal of its backcourt. The Celtics made the NBA Finals in each of Sharman's final five seasons, winning four. During that run, "Bull's-eye Bill" continued to hone his shooting touch. And his competitive fires never banked. Lakers icon (and NBA logo) Jerry West, whose first season coincided with Sharman's last, found that out the hard way. One game, after West had hit several jumpers in succession, Sharman decided he would compensate for his diminished foot speed by using his fists. "You did not drive by him," West said. "He got into more fights than Mike Tyson."

Sharman scrapped right to the end. He averaged 20 points a game against Syracuse in the 1961 Eastern Division Finals before the Celtics dispatched the Hawks in five games to win the title.

After the Finals, when he learned that the Celtics had placed him on the unprotected list for the NBA's expansion draft, Sharman promptly retired. He didn't want to leave the NBA as anything less than a champion. "He deserves the ultimate accolade," Heinsohn, his former teammate, said almost 50 years later. "He was a winner."

Sharman continued his winning ways as a coach. In 1971 he led the Utah Stars to an ABA title, then took over as coach of Boston's long-time rivals, the Los Angeles Lakers. In his first season the Lakers won 33 consecutive games, still an NBA record. More important, they won the NBA championship, something they had been unable to accomplish since 1954, despite a succession of star-studded rosters. "Sharman brought a more team-oriented concept," Lakers guard Gail Goodrich later said. Sharman, who died in 2013, is one just three men inducted into the Naismith Memorial Basketball Hall of Fame as both a player and coach.

70

Bill Cowley
Bruins Center, 1935–1947

Between the depths of the Great Depression and the height of World War II, the NHL contracted from nine teams to six. One consequence was a greater concentration of talent among the survivors—and the Bruins were an early beneficiary. When the St. Louis Eagles folded in 1935, Boston snapped up their promising first-year center, Bill Cowley. By 1939 Cowley was the leading scorer on a Stanley Cup-winning squad that featured ten future Hall of Famers. Cowley had just eight goals, but he distributed his league-leading 34 assists among a roster that included Roy Conacher, Milt Schmidt, Bobby Bauer, Woody Dumart, Dit Clapper, and Cooney Weiland.

But it was three assists to rookie right-winger Mel Hill that established Cowley as a Hub hockey hero. Each of Hill's goals broke an overtime tie against the Rangers in a grueling Stanley Cup playoff series—including the first Game 7 in NHL history. "The end came after exactly 108 minutes of play," wrote the *Globe*'s Victor O. Jones after the clincher, "with Bill Cowley recovering a wild shot of Roy Conacher's and feeding Hill a perfect pass."

Two years later, when the Bruins won another Cup—this time with a mere seven future Hall of Famers—Cowley was the NHL's leading scorer and MVP.

In December 1941, the Bruins' famed "Kraut Line" (Schmidt, Dumart, and Bauer) went off to serve in World War II. That gutted the defending Cup champions. Nevertheless, Cowley proved that he didn't need a Hall of Fame supporting cast to excel. He won a second Hart Trophy as the NHL's MVP in 1943. He was on a record scoring pace the next season when he separated his shoulder at Toronto in January. He missed 14 games, and the scoring record instead went to teammate Herb Cain, with 82 points. Still, Cowley set a record with 1.97 points per game that season. Since then only Wayne Gretzky and Mario Lemieux have surpassed it.

That 1944 season said something else about Bill Cowley. At the time of his injury, the Bruins were the third-best team in the NHL, and solidly in playoff position. With Cowley out, the Bruins lost ten of 14 and fell to fifth, one spot out of qualifying for the playoffs.

Upon his return, Cowley did everything he could to rally the team. In his third game back, playing through injuries to both his shoulder and his knee, he had four goals and two assists in a 10–9 win over the Rangers. That game set an NHL record for combined goals.

Just 12 days later the Bruins and Red Wings tied that record, in Boston's 10–9 defeat at Detroit. The loss mathematically eliminated the Bruins. Even so, Cowley's performance that night might have said even more about his grit than his Stanley Cup heroics had. With 2½ minutes left, the Bruins trailed 10–6. Fighting desperately to keep Boston's playoff hopes alive, Cowley put up two goals and an assist over the next 1:42 to make it a one-goal game with 47 seconds left.

That's the kind of effort today's Bruins fans hope to see. Even if you miss the playoffs, you should at least put up a fight.

Injuries, and sharing the spotlight with so many other Hall of Famers, kept Cowley from becoming a bigger star than he should have been. He was the NHL's all-time leading scorer when he retired in 1947. Inexplicably, he wasn't inducted into the Hall of Fame until 1968. He died on New Year's Eve in 1993.

69

Joe Cronin
Red Sox Infielder, 1935–1945

Poor Joe Cronin. Actually, Cronin was far from poor—and that was part of his problem. In October 1934 the Red Sox had paid $225,000—exorbitant by Great Depression standards—to acquire the All-Star shortstop from the Washington Senators. That created instant, if inflated, expectations in a town tired of losing. (The Red Sox hadn't finished above .500 since their last World Series win, in 1918.)

And now, just nine games into his first season as the Sox' savior, on Ladies Day at Fenway, Cronin was subjected to an unladylike display of venom. The Red Sox were playing Cronin's former team, the Senators. There were two outs in the top of the seventh. The Sox had trailed just 5–4 when the inning began. But Washington had broken the game open with five runs. The whole inning turned when Cronin dropped a throw from Sox ace Lefty Grove on a potential double play. It was Cronin's third error of the game, which contributed to eight unearned runs. Grove was now on the hook for the loss in a game he could easily have won.

But the worst moment, the thing that prompted the hail of boos, was when the 28-year-old Cronin, the guy who had made such a hash of things, had the effrontery to take the ball from the 35-year-old Grove and send *him* to the showers.

But Cronin was just doing his job. Because he was not only the Red Sox shortstop, but he was also the Red Sox manager.

There are no player/managers anymore. And even if there were, no one in his right mind would take on that dual role with the Red

Sox. Playing shortstop in Boston is challenging enough. (Have you recovered yet, Edgar Renteria and Julio Lugo?) Now just try to imagine playing shortstop for the Red Sox while also holding down the most stressful job in American sports: *managing* the Red Sox.

For 11 years Joe Cronin did both jobs and did them well. He hit .300 in his Red Sox career, with 119 home runs. He drove in more than 100 runs three times and made the All-Star team four times. In 1938, his best offensive season, he hit .325 with 17 homers and a league-leading 51 doubles. Defensively, he led the American League in fielding percentage twice.

And, with time, he gradually evolved from the overmatched kid who had trouble with some of the veterans (including Grove) to the respected leader admired by the younger players (including Ted Williams).

He also had the sense to put the team ahead of himself. In 1942, he handed the shortstop's job to Johnny Pesky, who ended up leading the American League in hits with 205 as a rookie.

Despite his reduced playing time, Cronin continued to contribute. In 1943 he had five home runs and 25 RBI as a pinch hitter, both American League records that still stand.

Cronin's playing days ended abruptly, just three games into the 1945 season. He broke his ankle while sliding into second at Yankee Stadium. But he was back in the Fenway dugout less than two weeks later, crutches and all. As Red Sox manager, he still had a job to do.

Cronin managed two more years, leading the Red Sox to the World Series in 1946 with a record of 104–50, third best in franchise history. His 1,071 wins as manager are the most in Sox history. After the 1947 season he replaced Eddie Collins as general manager. He concluded a lifetime in baseball by serving as American League President from 1959 until 1973. He was inducted into the Hall of Fame (as a player) in 1956. When the Red Sox retired his number (4) in 1984, Ted Williams told him, "No one respects you more than I do, Joe. I love you. In my book you're a great man."

68

Zdeno Chara
Bruins Defenseman, 2006–

If ever a defenseman created outsized expectations, it was Zdeno Chara. At 6'9", he was the tallest player in NHL history. He was also the Bruins' biggest acquisition when the team blew things up following a disastrous 74-point season in 2005–06. Bruins management wanted Chara to provide a presence not only on the ice, but also in the locker room. "They said one thing they were missing was leadership," Chara revealed at his welcome-to-Boston press conference. "I said I'm up to it."

Chara, a Czechoslovakian who spoke seven languages, was named captain before he'd skated a single shift. But it took a full season and a change of head coaches (from Dave Lewis to Claude Julien) before he really got comfortable in Boston. Then he was hampered by a torn labrum, which he played through in the 2008 playoffs.

But from the fall of 2008 to the spring of 2013, Chara finally lived up to those immense expectations. He was dependable, playing all but eight games during that stretch. He was impenetrable, winning the Norris Trophy as the league's premier defender in 2009. And, when called for, he could also be a formidable force on offense. He routinely registered the NHL's hardest shot during the skills competition at the All-Star break. And in 2011 he became just the fourth Bruins defenseman to score a hat trick, against Carolina—an accomplishment that he promptly brushed aside. "Playing good defensively—that's my job, to shut down top lines," Chara said. "I take more pride in that than thinking about hat tricks."

There was plenty for Chara to take pride in during the 2010–11 season. He was a key component in the Bruins' first Stanley Cup championship in 39 years. He had league-best plus/minus ratings in both the regular season (+33) and Stanley Cup Playoffs (+16). Tim Thomas (four shutouts, 1.98 GAA) was a deserving winner of the Conn Smythe Trophy as playoff MVP—but Chara wasn't far behind.

In Game 2 of the quarterfinals against Montreal, Chara was conspicuous by his absence. He sat out due to a virus—and his fellow defensemen committed three turnovers that led to all three Montreal goals in a 3–1 Habs win. That put the Bruins in an 0–2 hole as they headed to Montreal. Although he had lost ten pounds, Chara returned to the lineup in Game 3 and contributed a first-period assist as the Bruins took care of business in a must-win game.

Chara also came up huge in the second-round sweep over the Flyers. He had two goals in the pivotal Game 3 win, including a power play goal that ended an 0-for-30 drought in the playoffs. "Z's our leader," said Brad Marchand afterward. "And he showed he really wanted to win tonight. That's what you need—your leader to step up, and he did that." The sweep gave the Bruins eight days of rest—critical during a playoff run in which every other series went the distance.

Then, of course, Chara put a capper on his championship season by limiting Vancouver's high-flying Sedin twins, Daniel and Henrik, to one goal each during the Cup Final. After combining for 60 goals during the season, and ten more in the first three rounds of the playoffs, the Sedins were at a loss to explain what happened to their firepower. "Nothing has come easy for us," Henrik Sedin said before Game 6. "I don't know why that is."

The answer, a 6'9" defenseman, was pretty obvious.

Chara was a big part of another memorable Bruins playoff run, during the spring of 2013. It included the high of a Game 7 miracle against the Leafs in the opening round and ended with a shocking Game 6 loss to the Blackhawks in the Cup Final.

67

Dwight Evans
Red Sox Outfielder, 1972–1990

It was all-too-typical that a labor dispute bifurcated his best season. From his arrival, as a September call-up in 1972, until his departure, when the Red Sox failed to pick up his option in October 1990, Dwight Evans was denied his due by forces beyond his control. In that '72 season, the Red Sox finished a half-game out of first in the AL East. (Why a half-game? Because a brief players' strike canceled a handful of games and resulted in an unbalanced schedule.) His Sox career ended with Boston's tenth straight postseason loss (against Oakland), an indignity exacerbated by Roger Clemens's second-inning meltdown and ejection.

Halfway between, in 1981, Evans had what Peter Gammons called "a legitimately superstar year, statistically, defensively, and in the clutch." Evans led (or tied for the lead) in walks, OPS, home runs, and total bases. He ended with a Williamsesque performance on the season's final day, collecting two homers and ten total bases.

Unfortunately, Evans had his career year during a season interrupted by another strike, which obliterated a third of the schedule. It also resulted in a bizarre split season. So the AL East had both a first-half champ and a second-half champ. In Boston, the result was that fans had to endure the frustration of coming up just short in two pennant races in one year.

And that's to say nothing of the heart-rending endings in '75, '78, and '86.

No wonder Evans felt compelled to say upon his departure from Boston, "My only regret is that I was not able to help bring a world championship to the Red Sox and their fans."

Well, that sure wasn't *his* fault. For most of two decades Evans locked down right field at Fenway, winning eight Gold Gloves and gunning down runners with his laser-guided throws (he turned 42 double plays in his career). He also provided the kind of steady, all-around offensive production that stat geeks love today but was largely overlooked in Evans's time. Five times he finished among the top six in both OBP and OPS, and five times he finished either first or second in walks.

He had 77 sacrifice flies.

He also had plenty of pop. With 379 career homers, he's fifth on the Sox all-time list. And no AL player hit more home runs during the 1980s than Dwight Evans did.

Evans also came up big in big moments. He had four Opening Day home runs. He once hit for the cycle. His three-run homer provided all the offense when Roger Clemens had the first 20-K game in history. His incredible catch-spin-and-throw of Joe Morgan's 11th-inning drive in Game 6 of the 1975 World Series turned a potential two-run homer into a double play, keeping the score tied long enough for Carlton Fisk to work his magic an inning later. In two World Series, Evans hit .300 with three homers. In the epic World Series collapse of 1986, when Sox all around him were losing their heads and blaming each other, Evans had a team-high 9 RBI and hit a Game 7 homer that provided a short-lived lead.

But none of that was ever quite enough.

Not that Evans wasted a lot of energy brooding about what might have been. Once, when a reporter asked him for a postmortem on a typical hard-luck Sox loss, Evans brusquely rebuffed him. "Woulda, shoulda, coulda," Evans said. "I don't even want to think that way. I don't like that question. I'm not going to answer it."

In 19 seasons in Boston, Dwight Evans didn't have to answer to anyone. His play said enough.

Evans played 2,505 games for the Red Sox, second only to Carl Yastrzemski's 3,308. He was inducted into the Red Sox Hall of Fame in 2000.

66

Rodney Harrison
Patriots Safety, 2003–2008

His acetylene intensity was on full display. Rodney Harrison leveled a veteran running back, exchanged blows with a popular receiver, and got in the face of the face-of-the-franchise QB. And that was just in his first week of Patriots training camp.

It was 2003. Harrison, released after nine years in San Diego, came to New England with something to prove—to himself, if no one else. Maybe his full-on approach rankled Kevin Faulk, Troy Brown, and even Tom Brady. But it re-energized a defense that had regressed badly in 2002 after winning a Super Bowl. As linebacker Mike Vrabel later told the *Globe*'s Jackie MacMullan, "I remember thinking, This is exactly what this team needs. ... If I can play like this guy plays, I'll be on the field all the time."

Honed to a new edge, the Patriots' defense allowed the fewest points in the NFL over the next two seasons. New England won back-to-back Super Bowls—and Harrison was a big part of the reason why. As hardcore as his play was in practice and during the regular season, he found an eleventh level when the games mattered most. During the Patriots' 2004 title defense, Harrison had twice as many interceptions in the playoffs (4) as in the regular season (2). In that year's divisional round, Harrison had ten tackles (one of which forced a fumble) and picked off a last-gasp pass from Peyton Manning as the Patriots throttled Indianapolis and the AFC's highest-scoring offense, 20–3. "That's the way you have to play finesse teams," Harrison said. "You grab 'em and hit 'em in the mouth."

A week later, in the AFC Championship Game, Harrison had a backbreaking pick-six against Ben Roethlisberger just before halftime as the Pats rolled the Steelers in Pittsburgh. His 87-yard return—the only touchdown Harrison scored in his Pats career—made a potential 17-10 game 24-3 instead.

Next up was the Super Bowl, against the Philadelphia Eagles. Harrison needed no extra motivation to get up for that game—but Eagles receiver Freddie Mitchell foolishly provided some anyway. "Harrison," Mitchell had publicly declared before the game, "I've got something for you."

As trash talk went, that was pretty innocuous. What really fired Harrison up was when Mitchell said he didn't even know the names and numbers of the rest of New England's injury-depleted secondary. That showed a lack of respect not just for the Patriots—but also for the game. "Where's the preparation?" Harrison said. "What have you been doing? I've read the playbook cover to cover. And I know all [the Eagles'] names and their numbers."

The first time Harrison had played in the Super Bowl was during his rookie season with the Chargers. It took him nine years to get back. And in his return, in the Patriots Super Bowl XXXVIII win over the Panthers, he wasn't on the field at the end because he broke his arm.

Said Harrison, "I don't take things for granted."

Rodney Harrison went the distance in Super Bowl XXXIX against the Eagles. He had two interceptions and a sack against Donovan McNabb. His second pick, with just 17 seconds remaining, sealed the Patriots' 24-21 victory.

Freddie Mitchell? He caught one pass for 11 yards. And he never played in the NFL again.

Harrison's final trip to the Super Bowl, in 2008, didn't end well. He was unable to wrest the ball from receiver David Tyree on the infamous helmet catch during the Giants' winning drive. The following season showed the wisdom of not taking things for granted. The Patriots lost Tom Brady in the opening quarter, and Harrison tore his right quadriceps six weeks later. After 15 seasons, he decided to retire. Since then he's worked for NBC, and each year hears his name bandied about as a possible Hall of Fame candidate. Says Harrison, "If they vote me in, fine. If they don't, so what? I got Super Bowl rings, which is most important."

65

Nomar Garciaparra
Red Sox Shortstop, 1996–2004

At least Drew Bledsoe got to celebrate a Super Bowl win. Nomar, another Boston sports icon from that fraught turn-of-the-millennium time, was sent into exile just before the Red Sox' dramatic reversal of fortune in 2004.

And, in truth, it was time for him to go. His contract was up at the end of the year, and he wasn't coming back. The Red Sox had tried to package him in a deal for Alex Rodriguez the previous winter, which set a sour tone for Nomar's last season in Boston. Add a lingering Achilles tendon injury that had kept him out of the lineup for much of the year, and—well, it was clear that the relationship between the Red Sox and their five-time All-Star shortstop had reached the sell-by date. So the Sox dealt him to the Cubs at the trade deadline.

But to suggest that Nomar was never fully invested during his time in Boston is revisionist history. He captivated New England in his Rookie-of-the-Year season in 1997, with an all-out style of play (and a ritual of tics at the plate) that would have been impossible to fake. That year he led the American League with 209 hits, including 30 home runs and 11 triples (which also led the league). He set a major league record with 98 RBI as a leadoff hitter.

And he ran out every ground ball and popup, full speed. It was the start of a four-year run in which Nomar reached a level of performance and popularity that few other Sox stars have. In 1998 he hit .323 with 35 home runs and 122 RBI, finishing second to Juan Gonzalez in the MVP vote. He won the batting title with a .357 average in 1999, the same year he had two grand slams and ten RBI in one game. The next year he hit .372. That remains the highest Sox average since Ted Williams hit .388 in 1957.

But an old wrist injury that flared up during spring training in 2001 changed everything. Nomar appeared in only 21 games that season. And although he put up decent power numbers in 2002 and 2003, his on-base percentage, OPS, and defensive efficiency all dipped. That hurt his bargaining power under a more sabermetric front office.

It's unfortunate that his surly final season in Boston, followed by the surreal 2004 postseason, darkened Nomar's Red Sox career. If you want a more representative memory, think back to October 1998. Nomar got his first taste of postseason play, in the American League Division Series against the Indians. And although the Red Sox lost, 3–1, there wasn't much more Nomar could have done. He hit .333 with three homers. He drove in an ALDS record 11 runs—including the only four runs the Sox scored in back-to-back losses at Fenway. His solo homer in the bottom of the fourth in Game 4 gave the Sox a 1–0 lead that held up until the eighth, when the Indians got two off of closer Tom Gordon to put the series to bed.

Rather then sulk in the clubhouse after the Sox were eliminated, Nomar emerged from the dugout for a curtain call, a la Yaz on his victory lap in 1983. It was a display of mutual affection—Nomar applauding the fans as they applauded him. His message, he said later, was simple: "Thank you—thank you for being there all year."

Although he had one more All-Star season, when he hit .303 with 20 home runs for the Dodgers in 2006, Nomar never again approached the level of success he had in his first four years in Boston. But the bad blood of 2004 dissipated with time. In March 2010 Nomar signed a one-day contract with the Red Sox so he could officially end his career where he'd started it. The Sox then honored him with a day at Fenway on Cinco de Mayo, which paid tribute both to Nomar's Mexican–American heritage and his uniform number, 5.

64

Frank Brimsek
Bruins Goalie, 1938–1949

It was a Patriots-like move. Seven games into the 1938–39 season, the Bruins dealt four-time Vezina winner Tiny Thompson to the Red Wings. Thompson had turned 35 that spring. And for all their success in the regular season, the Bruins hadn't won the Stanley Cup since Thompson was a rookie, a decade earlier. They hadn't even made the Final since 1930. And despite finishing with the NHL's best record the previous season, they'd been broomed from the playoffs in the first round. The end was a shock; Toronto's Gordon Drillon beat Thompson with a slap shot from about 45 feet for the season-ender in OT. It was the fourth straight year that the Leafs had eliminated the Bruins.

Time for some new blood.

A minor injury kept Thompson on the shelf for the first two games of the new season, both on the road. That allowed the Bruins to test-drive a minor-league prospect, 23-year-old Minnesotan Frank Brimsek, with little pressure. Brimsek went 1–1 on the trip. That emboldened the Bruins to pull the trigger on a deal for Thompson.

Now the pressure was on Brimsek. Fans were in a panic. How could the Bruins entrust the season to a call-up goalie?

Thompson, in a classy move, offered reassurance before leaving town. "Don't worry about that kid," Thompson said. "He's a good man and he'll make them forget all about me."

It took all of three weeks for Thompson's prediction to prove true. In a span of seven starts, Brimsek had six shutouts—one of which was a 2–0 win over Thompson and the Red Wings. He played a stretch of 231 minutes and 54 seconds without allowing a goal, breaking Thompson's team record.

By season's end Brimsek had won both the Calder Award as rookie of the year and the Vezina Trophy. He finished 33–9–1 with ten shutouts and a 1.56 goals-against average. Once again the Bruins had the NHL's best record, 16 points better than the runner-up Rangers.

And this time, with Brimsek in net, they finished the job, winning the Stanley Cup. They won a tense Game 7 in overtime against the Rangers in the semi-finals before overcoming their nemesis, Toronto, for the Cup in five games. Brimsek allowed just six goals.

As the *Boston Globe* noted in an editorial, "The Bruins were mighty lucky to get two such goaltenders as Thompson and Brimsek right in a row."

The Globe *was right; the Bruins had a run of 19 consecutive seasons with Hall of Fame goaltenders. Brimsek backstopped the Bruins to another Stanley Cup in 1941, and he won another Vezina Trophy in 1942. He made eight straight NHL All-Star teams.*

63

Mo Vaughn
Red Sox First Baseman, 1991–1998

He was Big Papi before Big Papi. "When you grab a bat," Mo Vaughn once said, "it's [an] attitude. You have to look as fearless as possible."

Few batters conveyed fearlessness as convincingly as the Hit Dog. He was 245 pounds of menace, hanging out over the plate, waggling his 36-inch, 36-ounce bat like a matchstick, daring anyone to try to sneak an inside fastball past him. Orioles right-hander Jeff Robinson was one of the first to try it, on June 30, 1991. Vaughn, a recent PawSox call-up, blasted the ball 38 rows deep into the rightfield bleachers at Baltimore's Memorial Stadium.

It was his first major league home run.

Seven years later, Indians reliever Doug Jones knew enough not to challenge Vaughn. Jones tried to fool him with a changeup. Vaughn stayed back on the ball and whacked it into the rightfield seats at Jacobs Field. That bomb—part of a two-homer, seven-RBI day in Game 1 of the 1998 ALDS—was the last homer Vaughn hit as a member of the Red Sox.

In between those two milestones, plenty of other major league pitchers felt the Hit Dog's wrath. There was Troy Percival. The Angels fire-balling closer tried to punch out Vaughn with a 2–2 heater while protecting a 6–4 lead in the ninth inning at Fenway in July of '97. Instead the ball landed 435 feet away in dead center for a walk-off three-run homer.

There was Mariners reliever Paul Spoljaric. He gave up Vaughn's walk-off grand slam in Boston's home opener on Good Friday, 1998, when the Red Sox came from five down in the ninth.

And then there was David Wells, who started for the Orioles at Fenway on September 24, 1996. The big-framed, big-game lefty had surrendered just one homer to a left-handed batter all season. Vaughn took him deep three times in his first three at-bats. That put Vaughn in exclusive company. No Sox lefty had hit three homers in one game at Fenway since Ted Williams 50 years earlier.

The three homers also gave him 44 for the season, a career high. But the best part about that landmark 44th homer, from Vaughn's perspective? "It was my 200th hit," he said.

Vaughn wasn't a slug-or-strike-out DH. He prided himself on being a complete player, both in the field (he played first base) and at the plate. He reached the 200-hit plateau for a second time in 1998 and hit .304 in his Sox career. He even stole 11 bases in a season once.

But it was his awesome power that made him one of the game's most feared hitters. From 1995, when he was the American League MVP, through 1998 Vaughn averaged 40 home runs a year and 120 RBI.

Vaughn was also a team leader who believed in accountability. "You've got to admit your failures and see if you can learn from your mistakes," he said. On top of all that, he was a native New Englander (Norwalk, Connecticut). He was heavily involved in charity work, including the Mo Vaughn Youth Center in Dorchester. He wore No. 42 in honor of Jackie Robinson.

And yet Red Sox GM Dan Duquette let him leave via free agency after the 1998 season. Wrote the *Globe*'s Dan Shaughnessy, hardly an apologist for highly paid ballplayers, "Shame on the Red Sox for letting it come to this. Mo Vaughn is the heart, bones, and soul of the Red Sox clubhouse. … [and] he has made himself part of the community more than any sports star in New England history."

It turned out that Duquette's cold assessment was probably the right one. Vaughn sandwiched two years with the Angels and two years with the Mets around an entire season lost to a torn left biceps tendon. He didn't come close to matching the numbers he had produced in Boston, nor was he regarded as a clubhouse leader in either Anaheim or New York. He retired in January 2004 because of a chronic knee ailment. "Playing in Boston was the best time of my life," he said.

62

Doug Flutie
Boston College Quarterback, 1981–1984;
Patriots Quarterback, 1987–1989; 2005

H is entire career was a repudiation. Time and again Doug Flutie had to convince people to disregard what he wasn't and focus instead on what he was: a winner. Often his biggest obstacle was not his opponents on the field but the skeptics on his own sideline. It started with Tom Lamb, his football coach at Natick High. Lamb had heard that "there was something special coming along." But all he saw that first day was a 5'10", 160-pound sophomore. So he made Flutie a second-string defensive back.

First day of practice, Flutie's unit held the starting offense without a completion. Lamb still wasn't impressed. "But the same thing continued to happen," he said, "and after three or four days we couldn't overlook it anymore."

Flutie became the Bay State League's Sophomore of the Year as a defensive back. He was also a placekicker. And six games into the season he supplanted his brother Bill as the starting quarterback. After his junior year, the *Boston Globe* chose him as a defensive back in its all-star team of local high-schoolers. But as for his play at quarterback, the *Globe* simply noted that he'd been starting for a season and a half "and has yet to be replaced."

As a freshman at Boston College, Flutie began as the fourth-string quarterback. By Halloween he was the starter, leading the 2–4 Eagles against second-ranked Pitt and its Heisman-candidate quarterback, Dan Marino, at the Heights. And although the Eagles lost, 29–24, Flutie was brilliant: 23-of-43 for 347 yards and two touchdowns. Overnight, the city of Boston discovered that it had a budding college football star in its midst. And he was a likeable local kid of 18. "Isn't this the way well-made dream stories are written for juvenile readers?" the *Globe's* Leigh Montville wrote. "Hey, Doug Flutie outplayed Dan Marino. Doug Flutie outplayed everyone."

"He believes in everything he does," BC coach Jack Bicknell said. "He's flipping the ball around, doing some really goofy things ... and they work. You watch him and hope you don't coach all that out of him."

Flutie's approach carried him all the way to the 1984 Heisman Trophy. He took the Eagles to three straight bowl games. He beat national powers like Alabama (twice), Texas A&M (twice), Penn State, and Clemson. And he delivered one of the most electrifying plays in college football history.

November 23, 1984. Miami led BC 45–41 at the Orange Bowl. Flutie and fellow Heisman contender Bernie Kosar had traded thunder and lightning all day, each throwing for more than 400 yards as the Florida afternoon turned to a rainy evening. But with just six seconds left and the ball at the Miami 48—well, even Coach Bicknell didn't think Flutie could come up with something goofy enough to pull this one out. "I was thinking about what I was going to say to the kids after the loss," Bicknell admitted later. "I mean, you always say you're never out of it, but really ..."

The play call was 55 Flood Tip. Three BC receivers would sprint to the end zone. Flutie would throw to his roommate and favorite target, Gerard Phelan, who would try to out-jump the Miami defenders and tip the ball to a teammate.

Flutie lined up under center. No shotgun. Up in the radio booth, BC's play-by-play man, Dan Davis, had a measured tone as he began the call: "Here's your ballgame, folks, as Flutie takes the snap. ..."

Flutie retreated all the way to his own 35-yard line. Then he wound up like an outfielder on the warning track and *heaved*. The clock hit :00 as the ball left his hand.

The pass was a perfect spiral, deep, but at a trajectory low enough to slice through the wind and rain into the Miami end zone. Phelan was the only BC receiver there. There was no one for him to tip the ball to. It didn't matter. Flutie's pass descended over the outstretched hands of the Miami defense and hit Phelan right in the numbers.

Davis's tone was no longer measured as he relayed the result to his listeners: "TOUCHDOWN! TOUCHDOWN! TOUCHDOWN! TOUCHDOWN! TOUCHDOWN, BOSTON COLLEGE!"

And in his jubilation, Dan Davis summed up not just that play but also an entire improbable journey from second-string high school defensive back to Heisman-winning QB: "HE DID IT! HE DID IT! FLUTIE DID IT!"

Flutie played one year with Donald Trump's New Jersey Generals in the USFL before the league folded, and excelled as a CFL quarterback for eight seasons. He bracketed his stellar Canadian career with 12 mostly frustrating seasons in the NFL with five teams, including two stints with the Pats. Even though Flutie continued to win (he was 38–28 as an NFL starter) he could never shake his "yet to be replaced" status. The worst instance occurred in Buffalo. After making the Pro Bowl in 1998 Flutie guided the Bills to the playoffs in 1999 ... and was promptly replaced by Rob Johnson against the Tennessee Titans in the wild-card round. The football gods responded by dropping the "Music City Miracle" on the Bills, then inflicting the longest playoff drought of the new millennium. Flutie ended his career in 2005 with the Patriots. Coach Bill Belichick's going-away present was to allow him to become the first NFL player since 1941 to dropkick an extra point.

61

Dustin Pedroia
Red Sox Second Baseman, 2006–

There was little evidence that it was coming. In two years the Red Sox had fallen hard—from the euphoria of '04, to a first-round sweep by the White Sox in '05, to a midseason swoon in '06 (9–21 in August) that kept them out of the playoffs altogether. Holes appeared everywhere. Second base, for instance. Mark Loretta, a 34-year-old free-agent-to-be, clearly was not a long-term solution.

So why not give that kid from Pawtucket a shot?

The early returns were not encouraging. Dustin Pedroia, the 5'8" infielder from Arizona State, hit just .191 in 31 games at the tail end of '06. Nevertheless, the Red Sox awarded him the starting second baseman's job in 2007.

He responded by hitting just .172 out of the nine-hole over the first month. Pressure began to build not just on Pedroia but also on manager Terry Francona to make a move. The *Globe*'s Bob Ryan, speaking for much of Red Sox Nation (and all of Sports Talk Radio Land), wondered aloud in a column: "At what point will Francona decide that Dustin Pedroia is simply not ready to hit major league pitching?"

To make things even more awkward, utility man Alex Cora, a left-handed batter, was hitting .360. Why not at least go to a platoon system?

In one of his wiser moves as Sox manager, Francona decided to stay the course. "We don't want to pigeonhole a young kid after 45 or 50 at-bats," Francona said.

Just as important, Francona resisted the temptation to fiddle with Pedroia's unorthodox swing, which appeared to have too many moving parts: "I think that as a coaching staff, you can fall into the problem of, 'Oh, we've got to change him. He's at the major league level, he can't possibly do it like this.' Well, you know what? He can. We'd be wrong to jump in. This kid's pretty unique."

The evidence of that soon surfaced. In early May, four straight multi-hit games boosted Pedroia's average to a respectable .267. By mid-June, with his average over .300, he had supplanted shortstop Julio Lugo at the top of the order. He reinforced the wisdom of that move with a five-hit, five-RBI game at San Francisco.

He went on to win the Rookie of the Year as the Red Sox won the AL East for the first time since 1995.

How would the kid respond to the pressure of the postseason? When the Sox won three straight against the Indians in the ALCS after falling in a 3–1 hole, Pedroia contributed three straight multi-hit games. Then, in the World Series, he led off the bottom of the first with a tone-setting homer that started the Sox toward a sweep.

Pedroia followed up his impressive rookie year with the best season any Red Sox second baseman has ever had. He combined Gold Glove defense (only six errors in 733 chances) with Silver Slugger offense to win the American League MVP. "He is," wrote the *Globe*'s Dan Shaughnessy, "the most unlikely man to win this award in the history of major league baseball."

So how did he do it? He did it by hitting .326 with 17 homers and 83 RBI. He did it by leading the league in runs (118), hits (213, most by a Sox player in 20 years) and doubles (54). He did it by stealing 20 bases in 21 attempts. And he did it by playing with a perpetually dirty uniform and an amalgam of self-confidence and self-deprecating humor. Said Pedroia, "I'm not the biggest guy in the world. I don't have that many tools. If I'm walking down the street, you wouldn't think I'm a baseball player."

In 2008 he wasn't just a baseball player. He was the best baseball player in the American League.

In recent years Pedroia has been hampered by injuries that have hindered his effectiveness. But it's probably no coincidence that in 2013, when Pedroia played in a career-high 160 games, the Red Sox won another World Series. And in 2016, when he topped 200 hits (including a stretch of 11 in a row) for the second time in his career, the Sox returned to the postseason after two consecutive last-place finishes.

60

Adam Vinatieri
Patriots Placekicker, 1996–2006

Yankton. What a terrible town for a Patriots kicker to come from. It was a name ready-made for a classic New England putdown—like "Missin' Sisson," the nickname Pats fans tarred kicker Scott Sisson with in 1993, when he botched almost half his field goal attempts.

Just three games into the 1996 season, rookie Adam Vinatieri—pride of Yankton, South Dakota—was even worse. He had flubbed four of seven attempts, including three ghastly misses in a 17–10 loss at Buffalo.

And now, in game 4, against the Jacksonville Jaguars, Vinatieri missed yet another field goal, along with a PAT. The boo-birds emerged at Foxboro; an early 22-point lead evaporated and the Jags tied the game at 25 to force overtime.

The Pats drove deep into Jacksonville territory. A touchdown would have taken all the pressure off their struggling kicker. But Vinatieri *wanted* the pressure. When the drive stalled at the Jacksonville 22, he was thrilled. "As a kicker, you live for chances like this," he said later. "I got a chance to redeem myself."

And he did, nailing a 40-yarder to win the game.

It was the first of 15 game-winning field goals that Vinatieri delivered for the Patriots in OT or the last 10 seconds of regulation time. Three came in the postseason: in the "Snow Game" against Oakland in January 2002; against the Rams in Super Bowl XXXVI; and against the Panthers in Super Bowl XXXVIII.

But the greatest kick of Vinatieri's career—and maybe the greatest in NFL history—was the 45-yarder he booted with 32 seconds left in the Snow Game to force overtime. Afterward, the media expended most of its hot air debating the controversial Tuck Rule call, which allowed the Patriots to retain possession after an apparent fumble on their final drive of regulation. But that call would have become a moot point if Vinatieri hadn't delivered the tying three points under extreme duress. Said Pats coach Bill Belichick, "You can't get any tougher conditions than [kicking from] that far out with four inches of snow on the ground. But I had a lot of confidence in him."

By then, so did all of New England.

Along with the clutch field goals he delivered during his ten years in New England, Vinatieri scored an extra point with Pats fans the time he ran down the Cowboys' Herschel Walker and made a touchdown-saving tackle on a kickoff return. (YouTube it.) In 2018, as a member of the Indianapolis Colts, he set NFL records for career field goals made and points scored.

59

Frank Ramsey
Celtics Swingman, 1954–1955; 1957–1964

Red Auerbach's sixth sense about handling an NBA roster led him to create the "sixth man" concept. Auerbach was fortunate that his sixth-man prototype, Frank Ramsey, had the ideal temperament for it. Ramsey, "the Kentucky Colonel," was an All-American at UK. He directed the Wildcats to an NCAA title in 1951 and an undefeated season in 1953–54. He could have bristled at the idea of coming off the bench for the Celtics. But as a 6'3" swingman, Ramsey had the self-awareness to realize that it was the right role for him.

When Ramsey joined the Celtics in 1954, Boston already had the NBA's best backcourt, with Bob Cousy and Bill Sharman. After his rookie season, Ramsey spent a year in the military. He didn't rejoin the Celtics until January 1957. He had to play his way back into basketball shape on a team that now included center Bill Russell and forwards Tom Heinsohn and Jim Loscutoff, along with Cousy and Sharman.

Sixth man? Perfect. "I loved my role," Ramsey said years later. "When our guys got tired, I went in. By just sitting on the bench, I got a chance to see how the flow of the game was going and I knew what to do when Red sent me in."

The benefit of Ramsey's new role became obvious in the 1957 NBA playoffs. In the opener, against the Syracuse Nationals, the Celtics trailed 35–32 when Ramsey entered the game three minutes into the second quarter. The Celtics went on a 20–8 run, with Ramsey scoring 11, to take over the game. Ramsey ended up as high scorer, with 20, to kick-start a sweep.

Ramsey also came up huge in the last game of the '57 NBA Finals against the St. Louis Hawks, maybe the most intense Game 7 ever. The score was knotted at 103 at the end of regulation. One Celtics forward, Arnie Risen, had already fouled out. Boston needed a boost from the bench. Ramsey provided it by scoring the Celtics' first seven points of overtime.

The Hawks forced a second OT. Heinsohn, Boston's leading scorer (37 points), fouled out with three minutes left. On a night when Cousy and Sharman were a combined 5–for–40, the Celtics needed somebody to step up and hit a big shot.

It was Ramsey. He broke the final tie with a free throw, and then sealed the game with a 20-footer to give the Celtics their first championship.

Before sweeping the Lakers in the 1959 Finals for their second title, the Celtics survived a grueling seven-game series with Syracuse in the Eastern Division Finals. Ramsey, with 23.6 points per game, was their leading scorer. Playing with a splint on his right index finger, he scored 28 in Game 7, as the Celtics overcame a 16-point deficit.

That '59 title was the first of eight straight. Ramsey was around for six of them. By 1964, when he found his mind drifting more and more frequently to his construction business back home in Kentucky, he realized it was time to go. He averaged a career-low 8.6 points per game that season. But come playoff time, he dialed his intensity back up for one last push. His final game, as the Celtics closed out Wilt Chamberlain and the San Francisco Warriors in five, was a fitting end. With 18 points, the NBA's first "sixth man" was one of six Celtics in double figures. "He has given us everything he had all the time he was here," Celtics owner Walter Brown said afterward. "In the best tradition of the Celtics, he never gave up."

Although the Celtics offered him a front-office job, Ramsey walked away from the NBA for good when his playing days were done. He made a brief return to pro ball in 1970, as the coach of the ABA's Kentucky Colonels for one season. He was inducted into the Naismith Memorial Basketball Hall of Fame in 1982.

58

Richard Seymour
Patriots Defensive Lineman, 2001–2008

B all's down. Kick's up—and then it's right back down. Sometimes sheer size is all you need to make a play. At 6'6" Richard Seymour had size to spare. He used it to great effect, often batting down pass attempts. He also blocked four field goals in his eight years with the Patriots, including a 31-yard attempt by Tennessee's Gary Anderson in a 2004 playoff game that the Pats won by three.

Ball's out. Drew Bledsoe, the former Pats QB now with the Bills, has fumbled after a hit from Tedy Bruschi, who sniffed out an ill-advised naked bootleg late in the fourth quarter of a tight game at Buffalo. It's the kind of play the Pats' defense specialized in. While New England's defensive linemen occupied blockers—Seymour frequently got double-teamed—the linebackers shot the gaps and created havoc. It was the perfect scheme for a player like Seymour, who cared more about winning than about individual numbers.

But in this case Seymour enjoyed the best of both worlds. The ball was right in front of him on the Ralph Wilson Stadium turf. And, as Bruschi, put it, "Big Richard got it and took off."

Sixty-eight yards later, the Pats had a two-touchdown lead and the game was essentially over. Who knew such a big man could run like that?

"What is he, 310 pounds with quickness?" an anonymous opponent once told the *Boston Globe*, identifying Seymour as the toughest Patriot. "He's a freak of nature. If you don't seriously account for Seymour he can be awfully intimidating to your offense."

Gauged with the usual measuring stick, Richard Seymour was not among the NFL's elite defensive linemen. He averaged just under five sacks a season in New England. Use the only metric that really matters, however, and you get a much different impression. In Seymour's first four seasons, the Patriots won three Super Bowls.

Seymour began as a tackle in a 4–3 alignment but switched to a defensive end when the Pats went to a 3–4. "We take on the guards and tackles and hold them off," he told writer Ron Borges. "I'm fine with that because we've been winning. … What's important to me is that I feel I left everything out on the field."

So Seymour was content to expend most of his energy doing the thankless work in the trenches. But he was ready on those rare opportunities when the ball bounced his way—such as his fumble recovery on the Carolina 20 that set up the Patriots' first touchdown in Super Bowl XXXVIII. That play was largely forgotten by game's end, what with Janet Jackson's "wardrobe malfunction" at halftime and the two teams combining to put up 37 points in the fourth quarter. But that was fine with Richard Seymour. He knew the score, and the score was all that mattered.

Like many other Patriots stars of the Bill Belichick era, Richard Seymour left abruptly. A week before the 2009 season opener, the Pats looked at Seymour's expiring contract ($3.685 million) and his age (29) and dealt him to Oakland for a first-round draft choice. "Any transaction we make is with the goal of what is best for our team," Belichick said in a statement, "and as difficult as it is to part ways with a player of Richard's stature, many factors were taken into account when we considered this trade. … We are extremely grateful for the huge impact Richard's elite level of performance had on our success, and we wish him the very best during the rest of his career." In four seasons with the Raiders, Seymour made the Pro Bowl twice, giving him seven appearances in his career.

57

Fred Lynn
Red Sox Centerfielder, 1974–1980

He was too good for his own good. Fred Lynn set an unsustainable standard during his first full season in Boston, in 1975. He made the All-Star team. He won both AL Rookie of the Year and MVP. He won a Gold Glove. Best of all, he and fellow rookie Jim Rice, a.k.a. the Gold Dust Twins, propelled the Red Sox into the World Series for just the third time since 1918. Then the Sox pushed the dynastic Big Red Machine to a thrilling seven games. With a dynamic young centerfielder in place for the foreseeable future, Boston's fortunes looked brighter than they had in decades. What could go wrong?

Well, Sox fans got a hint in Game 6 of that '75 Series, which Carlton Fisk won with his 12th-inning walk-off. The Sox were alive in extras largely because of Lynn, whose three-run homer in the first had given them an early lead.

But Lynn had also caused Fenway to fall silent in the top of the fifth. The Reds had two on and one out when Ken Griffey Sr. launched a deep drive to center. Lynn, determined to preserve the 3–0 lead he had provided, chased the ball on a dead run. In the bottom of the ninth in Game 4, at Cincinnati, he had made a game-saving catch off Griffey on a similar drive.

But that blast had traveled 400 feet. This time Lynn ran out of room at the 379-foot sign. He leaped but couldn't make the grab. The wall had no padding at that time, and Lynn hit it awkwardly, with his tailbone. He went down in a heap as two runs scored and Griffey raced to third.

From then on Sox fans held their breath whenever Lynn tracked a drive in the outfield. "I took it personally when balls would fall in and I didn't catch them," Lynn once said. "But just because most of my injuries have come while I was playing aggressively, I'm not going to change my style out there."

Lynn's all-in, all-out approach was both thrilling and nerve-wracking to watch. Fenway fans admired the effort but feared the consequences. In 1976 Lynn lost 30 games due to nagging injuries, and his home run total dropped to just ten after he'd hit 21 as a rookie. In 1977 he got a late start because of torn tendon in his left ankle. He tried to play through it and hit a career low .260.

Lynn's most complete season was 1979. Having bulked up with weight machines in the offseason, he blasted a career-high 39 homers while also leading the league in average (.333), slugging, OBP, OPS, and OPS+. It revived hopes that Lynn could yet lead the Sox to a world championship.

Those hopes ended less than a year later, without warning. On August 28, 1980, Lynn fouled a pitch off his right foot. It smarted, but he stayed in the game—even reaching on a double to left. But his big toe was broken. His season was done.

As it turned out, so was his time in Boston. In January, the Red Sox included him in a multi-player trade with the Angels. Lynn, one of a disproportionate number of Californians to star for the Red Sox, was headed home. Gone was the man Peter Gammons called "perhaps the greatest Fenway Park player of modern times."

Lynn played for another decade, with four different teams. He continued to demonstrate sporadic brilliance (including the only grand slam in All-Star Game history, in 1983) that was short-circuited by injuries. But he was never able to replicate the magic he had created in Boston. As onetime Sox manager Don Zimmer once said, "Fenway and Fred Lynn seemed to be a perfect fit for each other." Lynn agreed. "You don't ever come to Fenway with a complacent attitude," he said. "You come there to play, otherwise they will let you know you are not living up to their expectations, and I liked that."

56

Wes Welker
Patriots Wide Receiver, 2007–2012

He was just what the Patriots needed. In 2006, New England blew a 21–3 lead in the AFC Championship Game at Indianapolis. With Reche Caldwell, Ben Watson, and Jabar Gaffney as Tom Brady's primary targets, the Patriots failed to convert four times on third down in the fourth quarter.

The upgrade at receiver in 2007 was staggering. The Randy Moss trade grabbed most of the headlines (not all of them positive). But a deal with the Dolphins earlier that spring proved to be just as important. The Patriots acquired Wes Welker, a rawhide-tough Oklahoman who had impressed the Pats with his versatility and desire. In his first game at Gillette Stadium as a member of the Dolphins, Welker returned five kickoffs and five punts. He also booted an extra point and a 29-yard field goal, subbing for injured kicker Olindo Mare. In his last game at Gillette Stadium as a member of the Dolphins, in 2006, Welker caught nine passes. No visiting receiver caught more that season.

All this from a guy who looked so small and slow that no NFL team drafted him. Before that he had received the last available scholarship from the only college to offer him one, Texas Tech.

He was, in other words, a prototypical Patriot. Mike Leach, his college coach, gave Pats' fans a hint of what to expect. "He's the greatest overachiever I've ever coached," said Leach. "People say, 'If only he was faster, if only he was bigger, if only he had longer arms.' And as they're talking he's making another great play."

With his two new receivers, Brady laid waste to the NFL in 2007. Moss did his superstar thing, stretching defenses and making

91

SportsCenter-ready catches. He had 23 touchdown receptions that year, still an NFL record.

But Moss didn't do it alone. Welker played a crucial supporting role. If defenses committed to stopping Moss over the top, Welker killed them underneath. He went over the middle time and again to move the chains, often taking big hits but popping right back up. His 112 catches that year led the league.

But Welker truly proved his value in 2009. Despite missing two early games with a sore knee, he still led the league with 123 catches. He also missed most of the season finale at Houston when he tore both the ACL and MCL in his left knee during the first quarter.

A week later, the Patriots entered the postseason without their prized possession receiver. They promptly suffered their worst playoff defeat in the Brady–Belichick era, a 33-14 home loss against the Ravens. Brady turned the ball over four times, with three interceptions and a strip sack.

Afterward the Patriots refused to use Welker's absence as an excuse. But everyone knew the score—including the Ravens. "With all credit due, it's hard to replace a Wes Welker," said Baltimore linebacker Ray Lewis.

Ravens safety Ed Reed agreed: "You aren't gonna get that same heart without him."

When Welker left town on a sour note, going to Denver (and Peyton Manning) via free agency in 2013, a revisionist history developed among some New England fans. Welker was never a true Patriot, the thinking went. Instead, he was a mercenary who took advantage of Brady's talent to get a fat contract elsewhere. That's nonsense. Welker averaged 112 catches a year during his six seasons in New England, and many of those catches ended with him taking punishing hits from linebackers who outweighed him by 50 pounds. "Nobody appreciated Wes more than I did," said Brady. "He's one of my best friends."

55

Luis Tiant
Red Sox Pitcher, 1971–1978

He's one of just two Red Sox pitchers in the last 75 years to make at least 38 starts in a season—and he did it twice. He's among the Sox' top-five pitchers in starts (238), wins (122), shutouts (26), innings pitched (1,774 2/3), and batters faced (7,289).

All of which would have sounded preposterous in 1971, when Luis Tiant arrived in Boston as an injury-plagued, over-30, Cuban-born pitcher who had lost 20 games with the Indians in 1969 and cracked his scapula with the Twins in 1970. After Tiant lasted just an inning in his first Boston start, the *Globe*'s Clif Keane wrote, "The latest investment by the Red Sox in Luis Tiant looked about as sound as taking a bagful of money and throwing it off Pier 4 into the Atlantic." Tiant lost his first seven decisions with Boston and finished the season at 1–7.

The tide turned, slowly, in 1972. Mixing a spot start with steady bullpen work, Tiant gradually earned manager Eddie Kasko's trust as the Red Sox made an improbable run at the AL East title. Kasko promoted Tiant to the rotation in August. Tiant responded with one of the most dominant stretches any Sox starter has ever produced. From August 19 through season's end he was 9–2 with six shutouts, including four straight. After his final shutout, against the Orioles on September 20, the Red Sox were in first place. Fenway resounded with chants of *Looo-eee! Loo-eee! Loo-eee!* The *Globe*'s Neil Singelais called Tiant "the most beautiful thing to happen to the Red Sox since 1967."

Although the Sox ultimately finished second to Detroit that year, Boston's love affair with El Tiante endured. He had three 20-win seasons from 1973 through 1976. Little Leaguers throughout New England mimicked his signature delivery, during which he shook his glove like a can of spray paint as he came to a set, then turned his back on the batter before delivering the pitch.

Tiant had first experimented with a hesitation windup in 1965, but didn't perfect it until he arrived in Boston. "When you get old you get smart," he said.

Back trouble bothered him in 1975, when he finished 18–14. But that was also the year that Tiant established himself as one of Boston's all-time gamers, with an epic postseason. He went 3–0, with three complete games in four starts. He beat Oakland 7–1 in a three-game ALCS sweep, putting the Sox in the World Series against Cincinnati's Big Red Machine.

By 1975, managers had already begun to lean on their bullpens in the postseason. There hadn't been a complete game in the World Series in four years. Tiant took care of that streak in Game 1, shutting out the Reds 6–0 on five hits. His stuff wasn't as impressive in Game 4, but in some ways his performance was even more so. Tiant threw 163 pitches—the last of which got Joe Morgan to pop out with two on to end the game and preserve a 5–4 Red Sox win. And he was the starter in the unforgettable Game 6, which the Red Sox won on Carlton Fisk's walk-off homer in the twelfth. Not a bad return on that bagful of money the Sox had thrown off Pier 4 once upon a time.

Tiant pitched three more seasons in Boston, ending his Red Sox run with yet another clutch performance. In his final Red Sox start, Tiant threw a two-hit shutout against Toronto on the final day of the 1978 season. That forged a tie with the Yankees that forced a one-game playoff, and also prompted Sox first baseman George Scott to declare, "In a big game, no matter what anyone wants to tell you, Luis Tiant is the greatest pitcher I've ever seen." But again El Tiante's heroics came to naught, thanks to Bucky Bleepin' Dent.

54

Ray Allen
Celtics Guard, 2007–2012

It didn't take long. In the second game of the 2007–08 season, the Celtics and Raptors were tied at 95 at the Air Canada Centre. Just 4.4 seconds remained in overtime. Paul Pierce inbounded the ball, and then stepped behind the three-point line. He thrust his hand in the air.

Nothing odd about that. Over most of the last decade Pierce would have been the go-to guy with the game on the line. But this time Pierce wasn't calling for the ball. He was celebrating. Ray Allen, having shaken free on a bruising Kevin Garnett pick, was wide open for a corner three, and Pierce found him. Pierce put up his hand in triumph while the ball was still in the air.

Said Allen afterward, "That was exactly how we drew it up."

Danny Ainge could have said the same thing. Over the offseason, the Celtics president of basketball operations had assembled a flesh-and-blood fantasy team. He brought in Garnett's menacing post presence and Allen's pure perimeter shooting to complement Pierce's all-around game. And while some might have fretted over this chemistry experiment—putting three alpha dogs on the same team—Pierce had no doubts. "With our abilities," the Celtics captain said before the season, "with our unselfishness, and the way we play, it's going to come together faster than people think."

Sure enough. The new-look Celtics won their first eight games and shot out to a 20–2 start. Their 66–16 record was the franchise's best since the legendary 1985–86 team. Allen, with 17.4 points per game and a team-high 180 three-pointers, fulfilled every expectation.

Until the playoffs started. Allen slumped during the Celtics'

20-game slog to the Eastern Conference title, hitting just 4-of-24 threes in the semis against the Cavaliers. Had he hit a wall as he approached his 33rd birthday?

The emphatic answer came in the NBA Finals against the Lakers. Allen rediscovered his stroke, averaging 20.2 points per game and shooting 52% from beyond the arc. He was at his cold-blooded best in Game 4. The Celtics came from 24 points down to take the lead. Boston was up three and had the ball with 26 seconds left and the shot clock winding down. LA could have tied the game with a stop. Allen, the only Celtic who played the entire game, pounded the ball at the top of the key, with Sasha Vujacic on him. Garnett came out to set a screen. Allen's response: "Let me take him."

Garnett retreated, and Allen blew past Vujacic for a left-handed layup that punctuated the greatest comeback in Finals history.

But the Lakers rallied to win Game 5, forcing the series back to Boston.

Allen remained in LA, where his 17-month-old son, Walker, had been hospitalized. Walker was diagnosed with juvenile diabetes. Allen then returned to Boston on his own, arriving via the redeye on the morning of Game 6. "I didn't even ask him about basketball," Celtic coach Doc Rivers said later. "I just asked him how he was doing. He said he was fine. That's all I needed to know."

Allen ended up getting a long rest in the first half—but only because Lamar Odom inadvertently poked him in the eye.

No matter. Allen brushed off the distractions, the fatigue, and the blurred vision for a team-high 26 points, including a record-tying seven threes. Four came in the fourth quarter, as the Celtics had their most convincing clincher ever, destroying the Lakers 131–92. "It's such a wonderful feeling to be able to do this on this night with all the stuff that has taken place over the weekend," Allen said when it was all over, and he'd won his first NBA title in his twelfth season. "And to be able to share this with the fans in Boston has been great."

Allen never got to share another championship with Celtics fans during his five years in Boston. But after taking his talents to South Beach, he played a huge part in the Miami Heat's 2013 title, nailing the tying three with five seconds left in Game Six against the Spurs on one of the greatest clutch shots in NBA history.

53

Dit Clapper
Bruins Right Winger/Defenseman, 1927–1947

Back in Hastings, Ontario, he was nothing special—and that's how he liked it. "When I get home, my friends don't ask me anything about the Bruins," he once said. "All they'll ask is, 'Where have you been all winter, Dit?'"

For more than two decades the answer was Boston. Dit Clapper was a Hub hockey mainstay, from his arrival in 1926 until his abrupt departure in 1949. He started as a minor leaguer with the Can-Am League's Boston Tigers and ended as an NHL head coach. In between he played 20 seasons for the Bruins, establishing a raft of firsts. Among them: first NHL player to be named an All-Star at both forward and defenseman; first Bruin inducted into the Hockey Hall of Fame; first player named to the Hall while still active; first (and only) Bruin to be a player/coach—and, most important, first (and only) player to win three Stanley Cups as a Bruin.

"One of Dit's biggest assets," said his first coach, Art Ross, "is his ability to absorb lessons from others." Another asset was his willingness to apply what he learned in ways that best served the team. At 6'2" and 200 pounds, Clapper was an imposing defenseman. But Ross converted him to a right-winger. Good move; in his second season, Clapper helped the Bruins to their first Stanley Cup. The next year, he teamed with Dutch Gainor and Cooney Weiland to form the "Dynamite Line." In their first year together, 1929–30, the trio produced 102 of the team's 179 goals. That team also posted a points percentage of .875, which remains the highest in NHL history. Said Clapper, "I guess we were a pretty fair sort of line."

But like all those Red Sox teams through the years that couldn't convert an explosive offense into a championship, the Dynamite Line fell short of producing a second Cup. So in 1938, Clapper willingly switched back to defenseman. Another good move; the Bruins won the Stanley Cup in 1939 and '41.

Clapper's well-rounded game included a reputation as one of hockey's most efficient fighters. Legend has it that he once scored a unique hat trick by dropping three Ottawa Senators in quick succession, each with one punch, during a brawl. And he added a conventional hat trick (along with a fighting major) in the Bruins' 8–0 drubbing of the Philadelphia Quakers during the infamous Christmas night brawl at the Garden in 1930.

Clapper was pressed into service as player/coach for the first time on February 1, 1944, when Ross became incapacitated due to neuritis. Clapper became a full-time player/coach in 1945 and continued in that role until February 1947, when he relinquished the *player* portion of the job. By then he'd spent half his 40 years in a Bruins uniform. He stayed on as Bruins coach for two more seasons and did a creditable job (102–88–40 overall). Still, he decided in the spring of 1949 that the job wasn't for him. "To be a really good coach you have to drive the guys," he said. "I couldn't really do that because I like them too much."

His fellow Bruins returned that sentiment. When Clapper died in 1978, former teammate Milt Schmidt remembered him with this: "I never met a nicer person. He was tough on the ice but so quiet and gentle off it."

52

Johnny Damon
Red Sox Centerfielder, 2002–2005

Between his Baseball Jesus look and his Jeff Spicoli delivery, it would have been easy to dismiss Johnny Damon as a legitimate idiot and not just the self-deprecating kind. But only a legitimate idiot would do that.

Damon was a huge part of the 2004 Red Sox' Magical History Tour. Batting out of the leadoff spot, he hit .304 with 20 homers and 94 RBI that season.

Equally important, he ground out at-bats and ground down the opposing starter—flicking his bat, spoiling pitches. "I want the hitter coming up behind me to get a good pitch to hit," he said.

The value of Damon's approach was evident during the Sox' storied comeback from a 3–0 deficit against the Yankees in the 2004 ALCS. Over the first six games Damon was just 3–for–29. But the Yankees staff had to throw 136 pitches to get those results.

Sixteen of those pitches came in Damon's final at-bat against Jon Lieber in Game 2. This on a night when Lieber needed no more than 11 pitches to get through any other single *inning*. And although the Red Sox lost that game, they learned something from Damon's approach. Facing Lieber again in Game 6, Damon began the game with a ten-pitch at-bat. The rest of the lineup followed suit by showing more patience. By the time Lieber left in the eighth, trailing 4–1, he had thrown 127 pitches—45 more than he had in Game 2.

Damon's plate discipline produced a much more dramatic result in Game 7. Trailing 2–0 in the top of the second, the Yankees' Javier Vazquez faced Damon with the bases loaded and one out. Undoubtedly aware of Damon's ability to go deep into counts, Vazquez left a first-pitch fastball over the heart of the plate. Damon crushed it for a grand slam. Next time around, Vazquez threw another first-pitch strike—and Damon crushed it again, for a two-run homer. Those six early runs killed off whatever fight the Yankees had left.

If the 2004 postseason showcased Damon's high baseball IQ, the 2003 postseason demonstrated his physical and mental toughness. Damon played an integral role as the Red Sox rallied from a 2–0 hole in the ALDS to beat the A's in five games. He hit .316 in the series, with a crucial two-run homer in Game 4. He also walked and scored on Manny Ramirez's go-ahead three-run homer in Game 5.

But he wasn't around for the postgame celebration. He'd left Oakland Coliseum in an ambulance. Damon was sprinting after a popup in shallow center in the seventh inning when he collided with second baseman Damian Jackson, who was also pursuing the popup. The collision looked like a vicious helmet-to-helmet hit in football. But this was baseball, and neither player was wearing a helmet. The top of Jackson's head struck Damon's right temple. (FSN's *SportScience* later estimated that the impact was equivalent to being hit with a 180-mph fastball.) Damon suffered a severe concussion that knocked him out before he'd even hit the ground. As he was carried off on a stretcher, he thought he still played for the A's—a team he'd left two years earlier.

Given today's more sophisticated concussion protocols, Damon would have been shut down for the rest of the postseason. Instead, he was back in the lineup just five days later, for Game 3 of the ALCS against the Yankees. In addition to his concussion symptoms, he was suffering from a severely bruised left arm—a result, he said, of a botched IV line insertion.

The Yankees' Game 3 starter was Roger Clemens. Damon went 3-for-3 against him.

As Damon later wrote in *Idiot*, his autobiography, "You just can't ask out of big games."

Damon left Boston after the 2005 season and signed with the Yankees, a move that brought upon him the full wrath of Red Sox Nation. Damon didn't understand the reaction. "Are people going to suddenly forget we won a World Series championship two years ago?" he said. "Or that I played with a concussion when I couldn't see right for months?"

51

Matt Light
Patriots Left Tackle, 2001–2011

No other pro athlete's job feels more like a job than an offensive lineman's. You can log an exhausting afternoon's work, on national television, and remain anonymous.

Unless you make a mistake. If your man beats you and takes Tom Brady down, suddenly everybody knows your name. And not in that pleasant *Cheers* sort of way.

Such thankless work isn't for everybody. But Matt Light signed up for it after his freshman year at Purdue. He had been playing tight end, but switched positions based on some simple feedback from his coaches: "They told me I could be an average tight end or a very good offensive lineman."

Light became a left tackle, which carried the added responsibility of protecting the quarterback's blind side. He protected his QB at Purdue, Drew Brees, well enough to draw interest from the Patriots, who acquired him in 2001. He became New England's first rookie to start at left tackle since 1968.

The Pats won three Super Bowls in Light's first four seasons, despite his being diagnosed with Crohn's disease. Pats fans never knew it at the time, but Light's symptoms became so severe that he collapsed during the offseason in 2004 and was rushed to emergency surgery. He had his appendix and a portion of his intestine removed. He was hospitalized for a month and lost 50 pounds. While he was recovering, his wife, Susie, picked up his second Super Bowl ring and brought it to his hospital room. "I thought, I have to get back and try to win another one of those," Light later recalled.

Less than a year later, he had that third ring. And he hadn't missed a single game.

During his 11 seasons with the Patriots Light provided leadership and continuity through the steady turnover that comes with offensive line play. By 2005, he was the only starting offensive lineman left from the 2001 Super Bowl team. Said Logan Mankins, who joined Light on the left side of the line that season, "The way he carried himself and the way he played and the way he worked out and trained, it's easy to look at someone like Matt and follow him."

Light also adapted to ever-changing offensive schemes and coordinators. He was a mainstay on the bruising line that led Corey Dillon to a franchise record 1,625 yards rushing in 2004, just as he was a cornerstone on the line that kept the pocket clean while Tom Brady unleashed a record-shattering aerial attack in 2007.

And while Light didn't always agree with Bill Belichick's methods, he bought into his philosophy to an extent that few others did. "It's always 'Do your job,'" Light said upon his retirement in 2012. "We hear it 5,000 times a week. ... 'Make it part of your routine. Keep striving to do it better and better.' So I think that the excellence that we all shared as an organization, teammates, friends, and everything else—it's not just an act. It's a habit. It's how we try to live our lives."

Three years into his retirement, Light was still doing his job and protecting Tom Brady. When the Deflategate saga exploded, so did Light, who called the allegations against Brady a "ridiculous circus that Roger Goodell and the rest of his little buddies in the league office put together."

50

Dennis Johnson
Celtics Guard, 1983–1990

It was one of the defining plays of Larry Bird's career. But he didn't do it alone. If Bird hadn't had someone to pass the ball to, his famous act of larceny against the Detroit Pistons in the 1987 Eastern Conference Finals would have been for naught.

That someone was Dennis Johnson. "He made the play, to tell the truth," Bird once said.

That's an overstatement. Still, like Bird, Johnson made a move that was both alert and athletic. And it transformed a looming one-point loss into a booming one-point win in Game 5.

Detroit led 107–106 with five seconds left when the play started. Isiah Thomas lobbed an entry pass. His target, Bill Laimbeer, stood like a statue along the baseline to the left of the Detroit basket. Bird saw the pass coming. He got a hand on the ball and tipped it away. By the time he got control, his momentum had carried him to the end line. He was off balance and angled too far behind the backboard to get a clean shot. He saw a white-and-green uniform flashing to the basket and fired the ball in that direction. "After I threw it," Bird told NBA. com, "I go, 'Oh, it's D.J.'"

Of course it was. Dennis Johnson, displaying the basketball intelligence that made him a key part of those great 1980s Celtics teams, read the situation and reacted. When Thomas inbounded the ball, Johnson was beyond the three-point line and inching up-court. But as soon as he saw Bird jump the pass, D.J. turned and streaked toward the rim. He caught the ball cleanly and made a harder-than-it-looked layup, using a finger roll while fending off Joe Dumars.

D.J. had followed an equally unlikely path to become the player Bird called the best teammate he ever had. In Seattle and Phoenix Johnson was a gifted shooting guard, a clutch scorer who was Finals MVP when the Sonics won the 1979 NBA championship. But he also clashed with coaches. His loose-cannon reputation enabled Red Auerbach to pull off yet another of his legendary swindles, acquiring Johnson from Phoenix for center Rick Robey in 1983.

The Celtics already had plenty of scorers. What they needed was a defensive stopper in the backcourt. D.J., a perennial member of the NBA's All-Defensive Team, was ideal. In Boston he also completed a career-long transition from shooting guard to point guard, averaging more than twice as many assists per game with the Celtics as with the Sonics. And while Johnson was never a great perimeter shooter—he made just 44 threes during his seven years in Boston—he was adept at getting to the rim.

The Celtics won two NBA titles in D.J.'s first three years in Boston. And it's safe to say they wouldn't have won the 1984 NBA Finals without him. Johnson led the Celtics in assists and was second only to Bird in scoring as the Celtics beat the Lakers in seven.

The series turned in Game 4. The Celtics were down 2–1 in the series and down ten at the half in LA. Then Johnson and Gerald Henderson decided on their own to switch defensive assignments. D.J. would take the much tougher task of guarding Magic Johnson.

The Celtics rallied for a critical road win as Magic committed five second-half turnovers. D.J. guarded him for the rest of the series, and the drop-off in Magic's efficiency was striking. In the first three games Magic shot 61% from the floor while averaging three turnovers a game. In the last three games, he shot 44% from the floor while averaging five turnovers a game. D.J. also harassed him into several mental errors that didn't show up in the box score.

Little wonder that Bird respected D.J. so much—or that Magic later called him "the best backcourt defender of all time."

D.J. retired in 1990 and had his number (3) raised to the Garden rafters a year later. He was coaching the D League's Austin Toros in 2007 when he died of a heart attack at just 52 years old. He was inducted into the Naismith Memorial Basketball Hall of Fame in 2010.

49

Mike Vrabel
Patriots Linebacker, 2001–2008

You'd think they would have seen it coming. Halfway through the second quarter of an October 2007 game against Washington, the Patriots had the ball and a 7–0 lead. On second-and-goal from the two, Mike Vrabel reported in at tight end. The 68,756 fans at Gillette Stadium knew what that meant. But somehow the Washington coaching staff did not. At the snap, Vrabel slipped free and into the right corner of the end zone. Tom Brady found him for a touchdown.

It was the tenth catch of Vrabel's career as a Patriot. All ten went for touchdowns, covering a total of 14 yards.

"Mike always makes that play," Bill Belichick said. "He's always open."

Some perspective: Mike Vrabel, a linebacker, had more receiving touchdowns for the Pats than Reche Caldwell, Donte Stallworth, Aaron Dobson, Kembrell Thompkins, Brandon Lloyd, Shane Vereen, Danny Woodhead, and Curtis Martin, to name a few.

Two of Vrabel's touchdown catches came in the same game, against the Jets in 2005. Two others came in separate Super Bowls. This was not some Refrigerator Perry novelty act, reserved for blowouts. Vrabel's first Super Bowl catch—and just the second catch of his career—gave the Pats the lead over Carolina with just 2:51 left in Super Bowl XXXVIII.

Still, as good as Vrabel was as a moonlighting tight end, he was even better as a full-time linebacker. Take that '07 game against Washington. Along with his TD catch, Vrabel had *three* strip sacks. The Pats recovered all three resulting fumbles and converted them into 17 points in a 52–7 rout.

For good measure, Vrabel also recovered an onside kick that day. It's no wonder that Belichick valued him so highly. "Mike was a great player who played in different systems," Belichick said. "He played different positions. He played on offense, defense, special teams. He played tight end. He played linebacker. Honestly, he would play free safety in practice for us once or twice a year. … He had a real passion for not only knowing his position, but understanding the total game."

Vrabel had languished in Pittsburgh for four years before finding a perfect fit with the Patriots. His versatility and unselfishness were hallmarks of New England teams that won three Super Bowls in four years from 2001 to 2004. For example: It didn't show up on the stat sheet, but Vrabel's pressure on a blitz led Rams quarterback Kurt Warner to hurry the throw that Ty Law intercepted and returned for the touchdown that changed the course of both Super Bowl XXXVI and Patriots history.

The 6'4", 260-pound Vrabel was also one of the most durable, consistent players of the Belichick era, averaging six sacks and 50+ tackles per season. He also had 11 career interceptions, 13 forced fumbles, and five recoveries. A broken forearm early in the 2003 season was his only significant injury—and even that cost him just three games.

Those were the only three games he missed during his eight years in New England.

Vrabel's Pats career came to an unceremonious end on February 27, 2009, when he and quarterback Matt Cassel were traded to the Kansas City Chiefs for a second-round draft pick. Vrabel played two more years before retiring—at which point he surprised absolutely no one by going into coaching. "Mike Vrabel is as well-suited for coaching as any player I have ever coached," said Bill Belichick. "I have no doubt Mike will develop tough, intelligent, fundamentally sound winners." Vrabel became the linebackers coach at his alma mater, Ohio State, before making his NFL debut as linebackers coach of the Houston Texans in 2014. He became head coach of the Tennessee Titans in 2018.

48

Danny Ainge
Celtics Guard, 1981–1990

Some players feed off the positive energy of the home crowd. Danny Ainge preferred the negative energy of a hostile arena. "There's nothing better than being on the road and making a shot and just really making the opposing crowd angry," he once said. "That's the ultimate—that's the peak of playing in sports."

Ainge relished his role as a pest whose exaggerated gestures got under people's skin. CBS's Curry Kirkpatrick once led a segment with the question, "Is Danny Ainge the most obnoxious, most despised player in the NBA?" And Ainge did nothing to dispel the idea. "With all the facial expressions I make," he said, "if I was watching me play, I'd say, 'Hey, that guy's a whiner!' "

Sometimes even his teammates found him annoying. "One minute he's your best friend," Larry Bird said, "and then he does something that makes you want to beat the crap out of him."

That tendency to butt heads, with both adversaries and allies, was the outward manifestation of an intense inner drive. At Oregon's North Eugene High School, Ainge was a first-team All-American in football and baseball as well as basketball. He expected to be the alpha male on any team he played on. In the 1981 NCAA Tournament, he put Brigham Young into the Elite Eight with a coast-to-coast drive through the entire Notre Dame defense in the closing seconds. And by then he was already in his third year with the Toronto Blue Jays. (During his abbreviated baseball career he got two hits each off Luis Tiant and Dennis Eckersley.)

So when he joined the Celtics, belatedly, in November of '81 (after protracted negotiations to get out of his Blue Jays contract), Ainge expected to have a significant impact. But the Celtics, defending NBA champions, had four players destined for the Hall of Fame. Minutes—not to mention shots—were hard to come by. Bird used to literally tell Ainge to get out of his way during games. Said Ainge, "I was humbled right away."

After three up-and-down seasons, Ainge finally settled into a starting role, if not a starring one. Teamed with Dennis Johnson in the backcourt, and with the original Big Three of Bird, Kevin McHale, and Robert Parish up front, Ainge was a key member of the greatest Celtics team ever (and possibly the best in NBA history), which rolled to the title in '86.

During his 7½ years in Boston Ainge was rarely the primary option—although he did have a 45-point game against the 76ers when Bird was injured in December 1988. But even then he was a bit irritating, referring to himself in the third person: "What you saw Danny Ainge do tonight was kind of play like Larry Bird."

Mostly, on a team of superstars, Ainge was happy to play a supporting role and grab whatever opportunities came his way. He made 86.7% of his free throws. He hit 38.6% of his threes, a higher career percentage than Bird's. (And he led the NBA in threes in the 1987–88 season.) He put up the occasional double-double in points and assists. He had ten rebounds in a playoff game against the Bucks. And when the Celtics overcame Michael Jordan's 63 points to win in double overtime during the '86 playoffs, it was largely because of Ainge. He had 24 points, all after halftime, including the tying bucket at the end of the first OT when he drove past Jordan.

And through it all he was happy to be the focal point of opposing fans' disdain. But those who focused on his histrionics missed the point. "I'm living a dream," Ainge once said. "I'm playing in the NBA with the Boston Celtics. What could be more fun than that?"

Larry Bird, as usual, probably had it sized up right: "I think people boo Danny Ainge because they're jealous of him."

Ainge's relentless drive to win has also served him well in his stint as the Celtics' President of Basketball Operations. In 2007 he astutely assembled a new iteration of the Big Three, which brought the Celtics their first NBA title since that storied '86 team.

47

Bobby Doerr
Red Sox Second Baseman, 1937–1944; 1946–1951

On the first weekend of September 1944, the Red Sox were in an improbable pennant race. World War II had decimated major league rosters—so much so that the perennially pathetic St. Louis Browns led the American League. But the Yankees, Tigers, and Red Sox all were within range.

With Ted Williams, Dom DiMaggio, and Johnny Pesky in the military, Boston remained a contender almost solely because of Bobby Doerr. The Sox second baseman led the AL in slugging that season at .528. He hit .325, with 30 doubles, ten triples, and 15 homers, while providing his usual rock-steady defense. On one Fenway home stand, Doerr had six straight multi-hit games, including a cycle against the Browns. He had a walk-off homer that beat the Browns in extra innings in August. He contributed a first-inning triple that helped give the Sox a 5–0 lead over the Philadelphia A's on September 2, and a ninth-inning single as part of a walk-off rally after the A's had come back to tie the game. The win drew the Sox to within a game and a half of first.

The next day, the Sox were on the verge of giving back what they'd gained. They trailed 5–1 in the ninth. Doerr led off … and fouled out. Nevertheless, the Fenway crowd of 24,098 responded with a standing ovation.

They were saying good-bye.

After the game, Doerr—whose middle name, Pershing, paid homage to a World War I general—had to report for induction into the US Army. In his absence, the 1944 Red Sox finished 6–17 and faded to

12 games back. Nothing—not the nine All-Star selections, not the six seasons with more than 100 RBI, not the 2,042 hits he accumulated over 14 seasons, not the 414 straight chances he handled without an error in 1948, not his three-homer game against the Browns in 1950—better illustrated Bobby Doerr's importance to the Boston Red Sox. With him they stood a chance. Without him they didn't.

The threadbare Sox finished seventh in 1945. But with the war over and all of their stars—including Doerr—back in 1946, the Red Sox had one of their finest seasons. Boston finished 104–50 to take the American League by 12 games. Williams, Doerr, and Pesky finished first, third and fourth, respectively, in the MVP voting.

The Sox, of course, lost the '46 Series to the Cardinals in seven games. Most of Boston's stars struggled. DiMaggio hit .259. Pesky hit .233. Even the great Ted Williams, battling a flu bug and an elbow injury, hit just .200, with five strikeouts.

Bobby Doerr? He hit .409 and led both teams with nine hits, despite missing Game 5 with a migraine.

There was speculation that Doerr's migraines were a result of stress from his time in the Army. Some players, including Pesky, said that military service gave them a better perspective on baseball. "It affected me just the opposite," said Doerr, who was stationed in California, anticipating—but never actually called to—combat in the Pacific. "I'm more nervous than I used to be. I feel the pressure more. I can't relax the way I did."

When migraine-induced nausea kept Doerr out of Game 5, his greatest worry was that his teammates would think he'd quit on them. Don Gutteridge, who subbed for Doerr at second, scoffed at the idea. "Imagine Bobby, of all people, walking out on anybody," Gutteridge said. "But it's just like him to feel that way."

Doerr's loyalty to Boston was simple and unconditional. "I can't even think of another town I'd want to play in," he once said. "If the Red Sox traded me I'd think of quitting the game." After retiring as a player Doerr was a Sox scout and became first-base coach for the "Impossible Dream" season of 1967, which he called "the darnedest year I ever saw in baseball." He was inducted into the Baseball Hall of Fame in 1986 and had his Sox number, 1, retired in 1988. He was just five months shy of his 100th birthday when he died in November 2017.

46

Julian Edelman
Patriots Wide Receiver, 2009–

He's a proxy for the most rabid element of the Patriots fan base. That was never more evident than in the fourth quarter of Super Bowl XLIX.

The Patriots trailed the Seattle Seahawks 24–14 with 11 minutes left. Third-and-14 from their own 28. Under heavy pressure, Tom Brady stepped up in the pocket and fired a bullet down the middle of the field, past the sticks. His favorite possession receiver, Julian Edelman, made the grab—and took an immediate shot to the helmet from Kam Chancellor, who outweighed him by 35 pounds.

Edelman held onto the ball for a 21-yard gain and a first down. But he looked punch drunk. If ever a play called for a third-party concussion evaluation, this was it.

Edelman returned to the huddle before anyone could intervene. Four plays later, he made another catch, good for another 21 yards. That set up Brady's four-yard touchdown pass to Danny Amendola, which closed the deficit to 24–21.

Back on the sideline, Edelman was finally examined for concussion symptoms. He cleared the protocol—which was heavily dependent on self-reporting. On the next drive, he caught two more balls, including the go-ahead three-yard touchdown pass with just 2:06 left.

When it was over, and Malcolm Butler had made his game-saving interception, Edelman was asked about the Chancellor hit. He said he wasn't at liberty to discuss injuries. And that was that.

Edelman had given every last bit of himself for the team—and for Tom Brady, whose integrity was under assault in those early days of

Deflategate. (Edelman to Brady, after the game: "You're the greatest quarterback in the world, man!") And he did so, in all likelihood, at great personal risk. Then he stonewalled anyone who questioned him about it.

That's exactly what thousands of Patriots fans like to think they would have done, given the chance.

But Julian Edelman has succeeded by repeatedly proving that he can do things very few others can. Like make *another* clutch fourth-quarter catch to help win *another* title two years later, as the Patriots overcame a 25-point deficit against the Falcons in Super Bowl LI. It was the most memorable off-the-top-of-the-turf catch since Franco Harris's Immaculate Reception in 1972. And unlike Harris, who was running free in the open field when he grabbed the ball, Edelman had to dive for the ball and simultaneously fight through three Atlanta defenders.

"He's really as good a competitor as anybody I've coached," Bill Belichick said. "He's played slot defensive back for us, returns kicks, covers kicks, blocks, catches tough passes, runs the ball for us on sweeps —he does whatever it takes."

Belichick neglected to mention Edelman's passing prowess: His first attempt as a pro went for a 51-yard touchdown to Danny Amendola against the Ravens in a 2014 Divisional Round game.

A quarterback at Kent State, Edelman generated little interest around the NFL. (He wasn't invited to the 2009 NFL Combine.) The Patriots, who chose him with a seventh round pick acquired from the Jaguars, were intrigued by the possibilities he presented as the football equivalent of a utility infielder.

Edelman has repaid the Pats' faith with the most well rounded résumé since Troy Brown. He holds the franchise record for most career punt return touchdowns (four) as well as the longest punt return touchdown (94 yards). In 2011 he was an emergency fill-in at defensive back. In 2012 he returned a fumble 22 yards for a touchdown against the Jets, on the kickoff following the "butt fumble."

But Edelman's greatest contribution has come at slot receiver, where he filled the void left by Wes Welker's departure after the 2012 season. To that point Edelman had just 69 receptions in four years; in 2013 he had 105, good for 1,056 yards. He had 92 more in 2014, despite missing the last two games of the regular season with a concussion.

He also suffered a concussion in 2012.

Edelman's head-injury history made his decision to stay on the field after the concussive hit from Kam Chancellor look that much more courageous. Or crazy, depending on your perspective. Either way, Pats fans love him for it.

The "Incredelman" catch against Atlanta was one of 21 Edelman had during the 2016 postseason, to go with the 26 postseason catches he had during the Pats' 2014 Super Bowl run. Add his 10 catches for 141 yards in the Pats' 13–3 victory over the Rams in Super Bowl LIII, good for the game's MVP award, and Edelman has elbowed his way into eventual consideration for the Hall of Fame.

45

Patrice Bergeron
Bruins Center, 2003–

What's your favorite Patrice Bergeron moment? The goal that put the Bruins up 1–0 at Vancouver in Game 7 of the 2011 Stanley Cup Final? The shorthanded dagger later in that same game, which dribbled past Roberto Luongo to make it 3–0 and obliterate any faint hope that the Canucks had left?

Or how about the one-timer against the Maple Leafs in 2013? You know the one. It came with less than a minute left in Game 7 of the opening playoff round and completed the Bruins' comeback from a 4–1 third-period deficit to force overtime. Or did you prefer the rebound he converted *in* overtime?

Or maybe it wasn't a goal at all. Maybe it was The Save. April 10, 2010. The Bruins led Carolina 3–2 early in the third. Seeing a delayed penalty call, the Bruins pulled goalie Tuukka Rask for an extra attacker. But down in the offensive zone, Blake Wheeler's pass back to Michael Ryder went wide and caromed off the boards. Then it headed toward the unprotected net. Here was one of those only-the-Bruins moments, unfolding in slow motion. An empty-net own goal, from the opposite end of the ice.

But Bergeron, who had replaced Rask as the extra attacker, skated full tilt toward his own net. He not only got there just in time, but he also had the stick control, using only his left hand, to capture the puck and sweep it aside, an inch from the goal line. You could watch hockey for the next hundred years and not see a better hustle play.

Or maybe it was The Fight. The first five-minute major of Bergeron's career.

There was some history there. In October 2008 Bergeron had suffered a severe concussion after the Flyers' Randy Jones drove him headfirst into the boards. He missed the rest of the season. He suffered a second concussion in December 2008 and missed another month.

So Bergeron was understandably sensitive about blind-side hits and cheap shots. Like when Montreal defenseman Josh Gorges drove him headfirst into the net after a goal late in the 2009 season. Bergeron filed that away.

Flash-forward to the second game of the 2009 Stanley Cup Playoffs. The Bruins were having their way with the Habs, leading 5–1 halfway through the third. That's when Gorges decided to pull one of those overrated "send a message" moves. He flat-out smacked Bergeron in the jaw. What would the gentlemanly Bergeron, a perennial candidate for the Lady Byng trophy, do about it?

Well, Bergeron not only fought back, but he also won, flattening Gorges with a couple of potent lefts. The Garden crowd roared, and his teammates banged their sticks on the boards in approval.

Or maybe your favorite Bergeron moment happened before Game 6 of the 2013 Stanley Cup Final against the Blackhawks at the Garden. The shock of defeat in that game, when a 2–1 lead became a 3–2 deficit in the final 1:16, was still a couple of hours away. Instead, there was only pregame euphoria over the sight of Patrice Bergeron in full uniform, ready to go. Just two days earlier he had left Game 5 at Chicago in an ambulance. Doctors feared a ruptured spleen. Turned out he had suffered "only" broken ribs and torn cartilage.

After Game 6 Bergeron returned to the hospital. On top of his existing injuries, he had suffered a punctured lung (either from the broken ribs or from a needle used in a pregame procedure) and a separated shoulder. He had absolutely no business being on the ice—but he'd given the Bruins 24 shifts in an effort that had come up just short.

Said Bruins coach Claude Julien, "There was nothing that was going to stop this guy from getting in our lineup."

Bergeron's old-school toughness needs no further validation. He got it anyway. In 2015, ESPN's Joe McDonald asked 97-year-old Milt Schmidt to name his current favorite NHL player. Schmidt, a Bruins center who had specialized in tight defense and timely scoring (sound familiar?) on a pair of prewar Stanley Cup champions, answered in one word: "Bergeron."

44

Vince Wilfork
Patriots Defensive Lineman, 2004–2015

Officially, he got no credit for the play. Officially, the infamous "butt fumble" was Mark Sanchez's own fault. Officially, the Jets quarterback simply lost the football after colliding with New York guard Brandon Moore's rear end. Patriots safety Steve Gregory gathered up the loose ball and returned it 32 yards for a touchdown. It was part of a 21-point explosion in a New York minute (literally) as the Patriots embarrassed the Jets on Thanksgiving night in 2012.

Unofficially, that play was all Vince Wilfork. And it was typical of Wilfork's contribution during his 11 years as a Patriot. He was a 325-pound presence in the interior of the defensive line, stuffing runs, clogging lanes, and occupying multiple blockers. Others often got statistical credit for plays on which Wilfork served as a wrecking ball.

So it was on the butt fumble. The reason Sanchez collided so hard with Moore's rear end was that Wilfork had shoved Moore—a veteran guard who had made the Pro Bowl the previous season—into the backfield as if he were chest-passing a medicine ball. And Sanchez, trying to salvage a broken play, ran right into him.

Even if the stat sheet didn't always recognize Wilfork's contributions, his teammates and coaches did. "A lot of times [his role] is to eat up blockers or try to disrupt plays," said Bill Belichick. "He's an explosive guy that's got very good football instincts. He knows where the ball is."

Wilfork showed that in another game against the Jets, on another fumble, in a January 2007 playoff game. New York was within a touchdown and had the ball at the Pats 48 late in the third quarter. On first-and-ten, Jets quarterback Chad Pennington tried a quick screen pass. Pats linebacker Rosevelt Colvin batted it down. Incomplete pass, play over. Or so everyone thought—except Wilfork, who recognized that the "pass" had gone backward and was a live ball. He picked it up and returned it 31 yards, setting up a game-changing score.

His athleticism surprised people. With 19 seconds left in the first half of a September 2011 game at Foxboro, the Chargers had a first down at the Pats 29. San Diego quarterback Philip Rivers tried to hit fullback Mike Tolbert in the flat. Wilfork got a hand on the ball and not only tipped it, but he also made a juggling interception and returned it to San Diego territory to set up a last-second Stephen Gostkowski field goal. And in a September 2014 game against Oakland, he grabbed another tipped pass for a game-sealing interception at the Patriots ten-yard line with a minute left.

But those plays were DVD extras. Wilfork's feature role was to anchor the defensive line. He did it well enough to make the Pro Bowl five times in his Pats career—a career bracketed by two Super Bowl wins a decade apart. When he won his first, against the Eagles in 2005, Wilfork was a rookie who was mature beyond his years. When he won his second, against the Seahawks in 2015, Wilfork was the defensive unit's unquestioned veteran leader, making one last run at a ring before the game's harsh economics intruded. "Few players reached or will ever reach the special level of Vince Wilfork," Belichick said a month after the Super Bowl when, as expected, the Patriots declined to pick up Wilfork's option. "There may have never been anyone at his position with as much strength, toughness, intelligence, instinctiveness, and athleticism. He is the best defensive lineman I ever coached, an all-time great Patriot whose place on our team will be missed but whose remarkable career as a Patriot will be remembered forever."

Wilfork wound up in Houston, surrounded by some familiar ex-Pats on the defensive coaching staff, including Romeo Crennel and former teammate Mike Vrabel. He played his final game, a 34–16 Texans loss in a divisional playoff game, at Foxboro in January 2017. The following August he signed a one-day contract with New England so he could retire as a Patriot.

43

Curt Schilling
Red Sox Pitcher, 2004–2007

In this case *gamer* is an unfortunate term. Brings to mind Curt Schilling's 38 Studios and the ill-fated $75 million loan from the State of Rhode Island. Just one of the many non-baseball headlines that Schilling has made in his messy post-Sox career. The contrast between his departure from the Boston sports scene and his arrival couldn't be more striking.

Curt Schilling was the perfect signing for the times—which were strange times indeed. November 2003. The Florida Marlins were World Series champions. Few people outside Florida cared (and not many people inside Florida cared, either). Major league baseball had become a high-stakes poker game, with just two teams left at the table. A month after the notorious Grady Little Game 7 in the Bronx, the dominant storyline was: What will the Red Sox and Yankees do next?

Boston's brass answered first, acquiring Schilling from the Diamond- backs during a Thanksgiving pilgrimage to Arizona. It was a surprising turn. Schilling, a baseball mercenary who had teamed with Arizona lefty Randy Johnson to beat the Yankees in the 2001 World Series, had initially expressed a preference for the Phillies or the Yanks. But he changed his mind. Why? "I want to be part of bringing the first World Series in modern history to Boston," he said.

And, he added, "I guess I hate the Yankees now."

That was chin music to New Englanders' ears.

Best of all, Schilling had the balls to match his bravado. He didn't shrink from the rivalry's intense heat. In his first game against the Yanks in a Sox uniform, he struck out Derek Jeter three times in a 5–2 win before 35,023 howling Fenway fans. It kick-started a season that surpassed what anyone could reasonably have expected from a 37-year-old power pitcher with more than 2,500 innings on his arm. In 32 starts, Schilling finished 21-6 with a 3.26 ERA and 203 strikeouts. It was a Cy Young-worthy season, even if he didn't win the Cy Young (the Twins' Johan Santana did). A pitcher brought in to fill the number-two starter's role behind Pedro Martinez had actually supplanted Martinez as the ace.

The Sox' pitching stars aligned for the playoffs. Schilling started Game 1 of the wild-card round in Anaheim, and when the potent Sox offense put up a seven-spot in the fourth, Boston's hopes looked as bright as the Southern California sun.

And then Schilling rolled his right ankle covering first on a Garret Anderson grounder in the sixth.

It seemed like no big deal. Until Game 1 of the ALCS, when Schilling gave up six earned runs in just three innings at New York. Turned out he had torn a tendon sheath in his ankle. After that Schilling and the Sox medical staff explored a radical procedure to temporarily stabilize the tendon in his next start. When the Sox fell into a three-games-to-none hole, the discussion seemed moot.

But after two stirring Sox rallies at Fenway, which made the series 3–2, Schilling and his surgically jury-rigged ankle staged an inspiring comeback of their own. In what became immortalized as the Bloody Sock Game, Schilling allowed just one run in seven innings as Boston evened the series. Schilling reprised that performance for the home crowd in Game 2 of the World Series, once again oozing blood through his temporary sutures while limiting the Cardinals to one run through six innings.

Schilling's ability to pitch through a serious injury added a level of drama that pushed the 2004 Red Sox into a realm approaching mythology. Boston had finally won a World Series, thanks in large measure to a mercenary whose socks turned out to be the reddest of all.

Despite a limited body of work (he made just 98 starts for the Red Sox), Schilling has a secure place in Boston sports history based on 2004 alone. But for good measure, he also won three games in the 2007 postseason, including Game 2 of the World Series. Fenway fans didn't know it at the time, but that was Schilling's last game as a major leaguer. He sat out all of 2008 following shoulder surgery before retiring.

42

Jo Jo White
Celtics Guard, 1969–1979

The good news for Jo Jo White was that he was the No. 1 draft choice of the Boston Celtics. The Celtics had just won the 1969 NBA title, their tenth championship in 11 years.

The bad news was that future Hall of Famers Bill Russell and Sam Jones, fixtures on every one of those ten championship teams, were retiring. How could a rookie guard from Kansas fill such an enormous void?

He couldn't. No one could. And no one, not even G.M. Red Auerbach, expected him to. "Remember, he is not the Messiah," Auerbach said.

Good thing White wasn't easily discouraged. As he said years later, when he'd finally joined Russell and Jones in the Hall of Fame, "I always strive to be the best. I tried out for the high school JV team and I got cut. So what did I do? I went out of the varsity team and *made* it."

By year two of his Celtics career White was an All-Star. But the true turning point came in year three, on January 21, 1972. It was a routine winter night at the Garden. The Celtics beat a bad Houston Rockets team 110–105. White was solid if unspectacular, tying John Havlicek for the team lead with 28 points.

What makes the game noteworthy in hindsight is that it was the first of 488 straight games in which Jo Jo White played—the franchise record. For six solid years he was an anchor in the backcourt. There's no overstating how important that was. Under Jo Jo, the Celtics regained their mojo. The year the streak began, the Celtics returned to the playoffs after a two-year absence. They wouldn't miss the playoffs again until the spring of '78—after White's streak ended. (By the way, add the 80 playoff games White played during that stretch, almost a full season's worth, and the streak is 568 games.)

In between, the Celtics were almost the equal of those Russell-era teams. In a five-year stretch they won no fewer than 54 games a season. The 1972–73 team had the best record in franchise history, 68–14. And the Celtics won NBA titles in 1974 and '76.

Like all great players, White elevated his game in the postseason. Beyond the better stats—21.5 points per game in the playoffs and 5.7 assists, compared to 17.2 and 4.9 in the regular season—White didn't flinch under pressure. In Game 6 of the 1974 Eastern Conference Semifinals, he ended the Buffalo Braves' season, in Buffalo, standing alone at the free throw line with no time left on the clock. And in perhaps the most intense NBA game ever played, the Celtics' 128–126 triple-overtime win over the Suns in Game 5 of the 1976 NBA Finals, White led all scorers with 33 points. He was also named Finals MVP, leading the Celtics with 21.7 points per game. "White was the one who killed us," Phoenix power forward Curtis Perry said afterward. "He made the big shots in a lot of games."

That was a common refrain around the NBA in the 1970s.

In retirement White suffered from the same unfair comparison to his forebears that he had endured as a rookie. Despite leading his team to a pair of titles and being named an All-Star for seven straight seasons, White initially received little support for Naismith Memorial Basketball Hall of Fame induction. Why? "A lot of people took him for granted," Tom Heinsohn, White's first NBA coach, said when the Hall finally admitted White in 2015. "He should have been in a long time ago." The irony was that, like Bill Russell, White was a team-first player who never worried about stats. In the end some of those old teammates, including Dave Cowens and John Havlicek, had his back, successfully lobbying to get him into the Hall. Said White, who'd had surgery to remove a brain tumor in 2010, "I'm still rejoicing from where I've gone to where I am to what I had to go through." Although he died in 2018, his Jo Jo White Foundation continues his mission of searching for a cure for brain cancer.

41

Babe Ruth
Red Sox Pitcher/Outfielder, 1914–1919

On July 11, 1914, Babe Ruth made the first of his 10,622 major league plate appearances. It came in the Sox' half of the second inning against the Cleveland Naps (now the Indians) at Fenway Park. "Ruth received a perfect ovation when he went to the bat," T.H. Murnane wrote in the *Boston Globe*, "and shaped up like a good batsman."

Ruth ended up striking out. Not that Sox fans minded terribly. At that stage, some 59 years before the DH existed, and in the brief period before he became renowned for his prodigious home runs, Ruth was a teenage pitching prodigy. And he delivered the goods. The Babe became an integral part of a Red Sox pitching staff that won three World Series between 1915 and 1918. Ruth won 89 games for the Red Sox—the same as Josh Beckett in his Sox days—and his .659 winning percentage trails only Pedro Martinez (.760) and Smokey Joe Wood (.676) in team history. And then there was his 3–0 record in the World Series, along with a 0.87 ERA and a 29⅔-inning scoreless streak.

So it's not a stretch to suggest that, had he continued on that trajectory, Ruth might well have made the Hall of Fame as a pitcher.

But he wouldn't have reinvented baseball.

In his first full season, Ruth's powerful bat began to overshadow his pitching arm. It was the dead-ball era; the 1915 Red Sox had just 14 home runs. Ruth led the team with four, in just 92 at-bats. His first career Fenway homer, on June 25, came against the Yankees. It reached the bleachers in right-center, making Ruth just the second player in Fenway's short history to accomplish the feat.

That set a precedent. The game's conventional dimensions could not contain this overgrown kid.

In 1918, for the first time, Ruth made more starts in the field than on the mound. The "good batsman" that Murnane had noted could no longer be denied. Ruth tied for the league lead in home runs, with 11. A year later he set a major league record with 29, even as the defending champs sputtered to a sixth-place finish.

Still the Red Sox continued to use him as a pitcher. The rising star—he was just 24—chafed. He arranged a lucrative barnstorming tour that fall, knowing that people wanted to see him thrash the ball, not throw it. And he thought Red Sox president Harry Frazee should reward him by doubling his $10,000 salary. A *Globe* account of the impasse ended with this: "Pres. Frazee did not see Ruth, nor did he have anything to say regarding baseball yesterday. He left at 5 o'clock for New York."

You know the rest.

For all the individual glory that Ruth achieved with the Yankees— peaking with his 60-homer season in 1927—he won just one more World Series during his 15 seasons in New York than he had during his five full seasons in Boston. And the Hub never got over its love affair with him. When Ruth made his first Fenway appearance as a Yankee, in a Patriots Day doubleheader in 1920, the crowd cheered. And when he announced in August 1934 that he would retire as a full-time player at season's end, 46,766 turned out for a doubleheader in his final Fenway appearance. "To that record crowd yesterday, hostile uniform and all, he still was 'Our Babe,'" wrote the Globe's Hy Hurwitz. "As the Babe walked off the diamond ... practically everyone in the stands stood up to applaud the stout, slow-strutting figure. 'It was a sight I'll never forget,' Ruth remarked last night. 'Boston has always been kind to me.'" While Hurwitz's report wasn't as artful as "Hub Bids Kid Adieu," John Updike's famous account of Ted Williams's final game in 1960, his closing line was eloquent in its simplicity: "The Babe has come and gone."

40

Kevin Garnett
Celtics Forward/Center, 2007–2013

He led the league in expletives. That, as much as the 15.7 points per game, the 8.3 rebounds, the 52% shooting, and the signature 18-foot jumper, was Kevin Garnett's primary contribution during his six seasons in Boston.

Not that the cursing was important in and of itself. But all those f-bombs were the outward manifestation of a competitive fire that burned like a furnace. Garnett's attitude and his intensity provided a nightly reminder that the Celtics' doormat days were over. He made that clear from day one. He put up 22 points and 20 rebounds in a 20-point win over the Wizards in his first game wearing the green. It was the first of his 29 double-doubles in that transformative 2007–08 season.

But Garnett's numbers didn't tell the whole story any more than his colorful language did. He was obsessive about the intangibles too. Like hustling to help a teammate up after a hard foul. Or swatting away every shot that an opponent tried to sink after the whistle. It was a borderline childish display, and yet it established expectations. *No letup.*

That attitude translated into results. The Celtics surrendered almost nine fewer points per game in 2007–08 than they had the season before. That translated into 42 more wins and Boston's first NBA title in 22 years.

And in Kevin Garnett's becoming the first NBA Defensive Player of the Year in franchise history.

Garnett deflected the credit like a telegraphed entry pass. "It's an individual award, but I won't take this credit," he said. "It's for the team."

But the team knew otherwise. "Kevin Garnett changes the defense," Celtic coach Doc Rivers said. "There's no doubt about it."

"You never know how valuable he is until you've played with him," said center Kendrick Perkins. "He controls the whole court. He's the only player besides Kobe Bryant that I've seen control the whole court.... He's very focused and he wants everybody else to lock in. He gives us our whole swagger."

Added Celtics captain Paul, "He's able to guard two, three, four positions on the court. He controls the paint. Blocks shots. He does a lot of things that don't show up on the stat sheet."

Pierce added one more: "Talking."

Garnett said he had a good reason to run his mouth so often. "You have to understand what's about to happen and then, obviously, speak on it," he said. "And talk loudly because sometimes you're on the road and you're dealing with [loud] crowds."

But Garnett also understood that there were times when you just had to shut up and play. Game 6 of the 2008 NBA Finals against the Lakers was one such occasion. Overall Garnett had had a solid series, notching a double-double in each of the first five games and playing his usual invisible-dog-fence defense. But his shooting had been substandard, just 35-of-87. And he had missed a pair of free throws late in Game 5 as the Celtics dropped a tight one with a chance to close the Lakers out.

So he came out gunning in Game 6. He had 17 points on 8-of-12 shooting in the first half, and the Celtics were well on their way to a 131–92 rout. Afterward Garnett's "*Anything's possi-bullll!*" was the sound bite in heavy rotation. But something he said shortly after that seemed more authentic. "I'm certified," he said. "I'm certified." Moments later certified Celtics legend Bill Russell embraced him.

The opportunity to follow in Russell's sneaker prints was a major incentive for Garnett, who bought into Celtics tradition to a degree that few others in recent decades have. "When you think of Bill Russell, the one thing you think about is defense," Garnett said. "I told him when I met him that I thank him for setting the tone, for setting the pathway for guys such as myself to be a big man and really exemplify excellence not only on the offensive end but exemplify it from a defensive standpoint. I tried to follow that lead the best I could through effort and hard work."

39

Manny Ramirez
Red Sox Outfielder, 2001–2008

Tough one. No other star Boston athlete toggled between asset and ass-hat as frequently as Manny Ramirez did. In 7½ years with the Red Sox Ramirez had too many "Manny Moments" to remember. To name just a few: Saying he would rather play in New York than Boston. Saying he would rather play in *Pawtucket* than Boston. Refusing to give up his scheduled day off, even after Trot Nixon got hurt and left the Sox outfield shorthanded. Refusing to pinch-hit against the Phillies. Pinch-hitting against the Yankees but refusing to swing the bat. Swinging the bat against the Rays but refusing to run to first on a grounder to the mound.

But then there was the flip side. Manny was an All-Star in every season he played for the Red Sox, hitting .312 and averaging 34 homers and 109 RBI a year. He was the MVP of the 2004 World Series. He hit .409 against the Indians in the 2007 ALCS. He ended Game 2 of the 2007 ALDS against the Angels with a mammoth walk-off home run. He had seven RBI in three games when the Sox swept the Angels in the 2004 ALDS. His three-run homer was the difference in the deciding game at Oakland in the 2003 ALDS.

If there was a single week that summarized Manny's time in Boston, it was the one that bracketed the trade deadline in 2005. That's the week Ramirez refused to give up his off day. He also failed to run hard on a potential double-play grounder late in a game in Tampa. Ramirez had been asking for a trade, and those two incidents seemed to push the fan base past the breaking point. When the Sox returned to Fenway on the final weekend of July, Ramirez was booed on Friday night. The Sox then held him out of the lineup on Saturday as they tried to ship him out of town before Sunday's 4:00 p.m. deadline.

Sunday's game against the Twins was Bizarro Day. In his major league debut, Jonathan Papelbon was the starter. Curt Schilling was the closer. And, once again, the best right-handed hitter in baseball was not in the starting lineup.

Intrigue regarding Manny's status added to the tension of a close game. The trade deadline came and went with no announcement. The game was tied at 3 in the bottom of the eighth. With two outs, the Sox had the potential go-ahead run at second. David Ortiz was at the plate. Adam Stern, filling in for Trot Nixon, was due up next. Twins manager Ron Gardenhire made the obvious move, ordering an intentional walk to Ortiz.

But it wasn't Stern who appeared in the on-deck circle. It was Manny. At the sight of him, Fenway's crowd of 34,929 began to cheer. The cheer became a roar when Manny grounded a 1–2 pitch up the middle for a single, driving in the run that put the Sox ahead to stay.

Before the next game, with his spot in left field assured at least through the end of the year, Manny emerged from the wall in left bearing a homemade sign that read: "The New Episode: Manny Being Manny." Then he went out and blasted a three-run homer against the Royals that propelled the Red Sox to a come-from-behind victory and kick-started another playoff push.

"Manny Being Manny" was renewed for three more seasons before being canceled halfway through 2008. Two incidents in particular—Manny took a swing at teammate Kevin Youkilis in the dugout and shoved Red Sox traveling secretary Jack McCormick to the ground during a trip to Houston—sealed the deal. The Red Sox shipped Manny to the LA Dodgers in a three-way trade. A pair of suspensions for failed PED tests, in 2009 and 2011, further tarnished Manny's reputation. He hit bottom when he was jailed for domestic battery in September 2011. After that, said Ramirez, "I woke up and looked at myself in the mirror and I said I needed a change. I started going to Bible studies." In 2014 he received a warm Fenway welcome during a celebration of the Sox' 2004 team. Ramirez used the occasion to apologize to Red Sox fans, saying, "Now I realize I behaved bad in Boston."

38

Jimmie Foxx
Red Sox First Baseman, 1937–1942

When fans talk about the greatest Red Sox hitters of all time, the conversation generally centers on lefties. That's inevitable on a team that was blessed with Ted Williams, Yaz, and David Ortiz. Maybe the occasional iconoclast argues for Wade Boggs.

Best righty? The knee-jerk answer is Manny Ramirez. You don't hear many arguments for Jimmie Foxx—but you should. For a five-year stretch, Foxx was as good as any hitter the Red Sox ever had—righty or lefty.

Go ahead. Look it up. Foxx was MVP in 1938, when he hit .349 with 50 home runs, 175 RBI (still a Sox record), an on-base percentage of .462, a slugging percentage of .704, and an OPS 1.166. The next year he finished second in the MVP voting. He hit .360 and led the American League with 35 homers, despite missing the final 21 games due to an emergency appendectomy.

In terms of attitude Foxx was the anti-Manny, as that bout with appendicitis illustrated. Doctors diagnosed his condition in Washington in late June, but Foxx decided to play through it. By a September trip to Yankee Stadium he was so ill he could barely eat. He continued with the team to Philadelphia, where he finally consented to season-ending (and possibly life-saving) surgery.

Foxx also struggled with chronic sinus trouble, possibly a result of a 1934 beaning in a barnstorming game. He developed a sinus infection during spring training in 1937. Headaches and blurred vision plagued him all year. Nevertheless, he sat out just two games.

And while he hit only .285, a career low to that point, he still had 36 home runs and 127 RBI.

Although primarily a first baseman, Foxx was no lummox in the field. During his career he played every position except centerfield. In 1940, at player/manager Joe Cronin's request, Foxx switched to catcher so Cronin could get All-Star utility man Lou Finney in the lineup at first. (Try to picture Manny doing that.) Said Cronin, "They can talk all they want to about some of those old-time ballplayers being able to play different positions. I'll take Foxxie. They don't come any better." (When he concluded his career in 1945 with the Phillies, Foxx made nine appearances as a pitcher and compiled a 1.59 ERA in 22⅔ innings.)

It's a shame so many modern Red Sox fans don't know Jimmie Foxx from Jamie Foxx. Few players were better suited for Boston. "I know, and most players know, that this is the most appreciative baseball city in the country," Foxx said when the Philadelphia A's sold him to the Red Sox after the 1935 season. At six feet tall and almost 200 pounds, Foxx was a power hitter with a perfect Fenway swing (35 of his 50 homers in 1938 were at home). Many of his home runs were majestic blasts, including a bomb in 1937 that went clear out of Fenway in *center*.

But Foxx was also an intelligent hitter who took what the pitcher gave him. (He once walked six times in a game.) He was also a team leader; he even managed a game during his time with the A's when Connie Mack was called out of town on a legal matter.

Best of all, Foxx helped make the Red Sox competitive again. The 1937 team was the first in 20 years to win 80 games. And when Ted Williams came along in 1939, the Red Sox had one of the best righty/lefty combos in the middle of the order that they've ever had—if not *the* best. As Williams, the greatest hitter who ever lived, once said, "I felt weak in comparison to Jimmie Foxx."

Foxx's power declined rapidly after the 1940 season. He had just 19 home runs in 1941. The Red Sox waived him in 1942 and he was picked up by the Cubs. He finished his magnificent career (a .325 lifetime average, .428 OBP, 1.038 OPS, and 534 home runs) with the Phillies. He was inducted into the Hall of Fame in 1951 and died of a heart attack in Miami in 1967, at just 59 years old.

37

Robert Parish
Celtics Center, 1980–1994

During his 13 years in Boston, Robert Parish played in more than two full seasons' worth of playoff games. He also played a pivotal role in three championships (in 1981, '84, and '86). The highlights underscore his all-around game. Game 5 of the 1981 Eastern Conference Final: Twice he blocked the Sixers' Andrew Toney in the final 90 seconds, helping the Celtics overcome a six-point deficit. Game 2 of the 1984 NBA Finals against the Lakers: Parish picked Bob McAdoo's's pocket with six seconds left in overtime and the Celtics protecting a one-point lead. Game 4 of the 1984 NBA Finals. With the Celtics down five in the last minute of regulation, Parish A) converted an and-one on a put-back; B) rebounded Michael Cooper's miss on LA's next possession, after which Larry Bird tied the game with two free throws; and C) stole Magic Johnson's entry pass to James Worthy with four seconds left to force overtime. Boston won 129–125. Game 4, 1986 NBA Finals: In 40 exhausting minutes against Houston's towering duo of Hakeem Olajuwon and Ralph Sampson, Parish put up team highs in points (22) and rebounds (ten). But he took a seat for the final 3:07 as high-energy super-sub Bill Walton closed out a 106–103 road win.

That unsung act—not grousing about being on the bench at crunch time—said a lot about Parish's attitude. "He was one of most dependable teammates you could ever have," Kevin McHale said years later, when Parish was elected to the Basketball Hall of Fame. "He was there for every practice. For every game. He very seldom missed anything, including assignments on the floor. His longevity is unbelievable, but his dependability was just as impressive. I feel fortunate to have played with him."

Said Walton, who delivered Parish's induction speech in Springfield, "He is exactly what the Basketball Hall of Fame is all about."

And yet for all the great plays, for the eight seasons in which he averaged a double-double, and for the high regard that his teammates had for him, Parish is perhaps best remembered for a single spasm of violence.

Game 5 of the 1987 Eastern Conference Finals against Detroit's "Bad Boy" Pistons. It had been a testy series. In Game 3, Larry Bird and Detroit center Bill Laimbeer had been ejected for fighting after Laimbeer took Bird down hard under the basket. And now, just before halftime, as Parish and Laimbeer jostled for a rebound, Laimbeer threw out his left arm and caught Parish with an elbow to the throat.

A couple of swings of Parish's long arms later, Laimbeer was in a heap on the parquet floor. The inscrutable Chief, quietest player on a team full of trash talkers, had just made a wordless statement: *We're done with you and your cheap shots.*

Did Parish cross a line? Probably. But he never much cared what anyone outside his own locker room thought, going back to his days at Centenary College in Louisiana. The school was on NCAA probation during Parish's entire tenure because it had offered basketball scholarships to five players (including Parish) who had used a testing service other than SAT to establish academic eligibility. The college could have avoided probation by rescinding the scholarships. Centenary refused. Because the school honored the terms of its scholarship, so did Parish. A bona fide NBA prospect, he spent four years playing at an obscure school that not only was ineligible for tournament play, but which also lacked any officially recognized statistics (including Parish's 21.6 points and 16.9 rebounds per game).

Parish ended up in the NBA anyway. And it was little wonder that he found a home on a team renowned for unselfish play. Walton acknowledged this in Parish's induction speech. "Some will say that Robert was lucky—that he played on great team with unbelievable talents," Walton said. "The reality is that *we* were the lucky ones to be on *his* team."

After leaving Boston, Parish spent two years in Charlotte before ending his 21-year NBA career in Chicago, where he picked up a fourth championship ring with Michael Jordan's Bulls.

36

Rocky Marciano
World Heavyweight Boxing Champion, 1952–1956

Sylvester Stallone could have scripted the moment:
Rocky was an undersized upstart who dropped out of high school after the tenth grade to help support his immigrant parents. He overcame infinitesimally long odds to earn a shot at the heavyweight championship. The title bout was in Philadelphia.

Rocky was in trouble from the outset. The dream seemed doomed. The champion had dismissed Rocky as an "amateur" because of his unsophisticated style. Rocky was a you-should-see-the-other-guy fighter. He got by with toughness and heart—a willingness to go toe-to-toe with anybody and try to land just one more punch than he took.

But the champ flattened him in the first round and Rocky looked dazed. He got up—of course—but as the rounds dragged on he took a beating. By Round 11 both eyes were badly swollen, and Rocky was blinking back blood. "He's badly cut," the TV announcer said. "*Badly cut. He's pretty near helpless.*"

He was saved by the bell.

The twelfth round wasn't much better. He plugged away—"Rocky rushing in, still gamely trying"—but by now he was so far behind on each judge's scorecard that his only hope was to score a miraculous knockout.

After Round 12 the announcer noted that the champ's manager was "very confidently talking to friends in the press rows." Then he added, portentously: "Now we go to Round 13. The unlucky number. Maybe."

Less than 30 seconds later, the thunderclap happened. The champ, perhaps as confident as his manager, let his guard down for just an eyeblink. Rocky responded with a remarkable display of fortitude and fast-twitch muscle fibers. He flashed a vicious right hook. The champ's head swiveled. The champ then slipped down the ropes and remained motionless on the canvas throughout the ten count.

He was out cold.

This was not a Sly Stallone fantasy. These events really happened, at Philadelphia's Municipal Stadium on September 22, 1952.

After a prolonged silence, the announcer on the closed-circuit TV broadcast, a veteran boxing writer named Bill Koram, spoke. "And Rocky Marciano is the…"—here Koram hesitated, as if he couldn't quite believe what he was about to say—"…heavyweight champion of the world."

Rocco Francis Marchegiano—early on he changed his name to accommodate a ring announcer whose tongue suffered a TKO—had spent his entire career overcoming doubters. It had taken him 42 fights to earn that title shot against Jersey Joe Walcott. Marciano had started late, boxing in earnest for the first time while serving in the Army at the tail end of World War II. He'd had little training. Boxing wasn't the sport he aspired to—it's just what he ended up doing when he washed out as a baseball prospect. But he had instant success, running up a string of 16 straight knockouts to start his career, with nine coming in the first round. By then he realized that he could literally fight his way out of the poverty his family had endured since his father had become a shoemaker in Brockton after emigrating from Italy.

Once he became champion, Rocky fought just six more times. He retired at 32. He'd seen what happened to other great champions who had hung on too long. (After defeating a faded Joe Louis—the victory that finally put him on track for a title shot—Marciano felt compelled to apologize.)

For all the toughness he displayed in the ring, Marciano was sensitive. "I don't mind knocking a guy out," he once said, "but I just don't want to hurt anybody's feelings."

And so, with his family taken care of, Rocky Marciano was happy to walk away while he still could. He was 49–0, the only undefeated heavyweight champion in history. "I am comfortably fixed," he said, "and I am not afraid of the future."

Rocky's post-boxing life was successful—he became a businessman and television personality—but far too brief. He died on August 31, 1969, when a Cessna 172 flying him to his 46th birthday party crashed in Iowa. Wrote Red Smith, one of the pre-eminent sports columnists of the day, "Rocky Marciano was not a skillful boxer. He wasn't fast or graceful or stylish. He was just one of the greatest fighters that ever lived."

35

Smoky Joe Wood
Red Sox Pitcher, 1908–1915

He set a high standard for the faithful in Fenway's first season. Red Sox right-hander Smoky Joe Wood won 34 games in 1912, a franchise record that still stands and always will.

Wood began his Sox career pitching at the Huntington Avenue Grounds. After three mediocre years, he had a breakthrough season in 1911. He won 23 games, including a no-hitter against the St. Louis Browns.

At first the move to a new ballpark didn't go well. On a frigid April Tuesday, Wood lost his first Fenway start, to the Washington Senators. On May 25 at Fenway, the defending champion Philadelphia A's pounded Wood 8–2. The loss dropped the Red Sox four games behind the first-place Chicago White Sox.

And then everything changed. Wood didn't lose again at Fenway for the duration of the 1912 pennant race. For the first time he consistently commanded the blazing fastball that had earned him his nickname (credited to *Boston Post* writer Paul Shannon, who said, "That boy throws smoke"). He lost just one game in 3½ months, a 4–3 decision at Philadelphia on the Fourth of July.

By the first week of September the Red Sox had a 14½-game lead. Wood's record stood at 29–4, and he had won 14 straight decisions. Washington's ace, the great Walter Johnson, held the American League record of 16 consecutive wins. Johnson was set to pitch the second game of a three-game series at Fenway. Wood was set to pitch the third.

Washington manager Clark Griffith issued a challenge. He said if Wood was truly worthy of beating Johnson's record, he ought to go head-to-head with the Big Train. Sox manager Jake Stahl accepted the challenge and moved Wood's start up a day. "And we will beat them, too," said Stahl.

Despite short notice for this dream matchup, a crowd of 29,000 turned out at Fenway on a Friday afternoon. For once, they saw a pitchers' duel that lived up to the hype. Wood and the Red Sox won 1–0, on back-to-back doubles by Tris Speaker and Duffy Lewis in the sixth. Wood ended the game with back-to-back strikeouts that stranded the tying run at second.

Wood tied Johnson's record of 16 straight wins before losing at Detroit. Then, in the World Series against the New York Giants, he won twice at the Polo Grounds as the Red Sox built a 3–1 series lead (there was also one tie). The Giants won to make it 3–2, but no matter: The Sox had Wood lined up for the next game, at Fenway.

Well, Wood did indeed beat the Giants at Fenway to clinch the series—just not in the way anyone anticipated. He lasted just one inning in his start, as the Giants routed the Sox 11-4 to square the series. But in the deciding game the next day, Wood came out of the bullpen in the eighth inning with the game tied 1–1. And he picked up the win, despite allowing the go-ahead run in the tenth, when the Red Sox rallied for two runs on a couple of New York misplays.

No, Smoky Joe Wood might not have deserved *that* win. But the way he had pitched throughout Fenway's first season, he deserved *to* win.

Wood, who once said "I threw so hard I thought my arm would fly right off my body," was plagued by injuries throughout his career. He missed the Sox' 1915 World Series triumph over the Phillies, after finishing 15–5 with a 1.49 ERA that year. Wood sat out the 1916 season, and then the Red Sox sold him to the Indians. He reinvented himself as an outfielder in Cleveland, hitting .297 over five seasons. He coached at Yale for 20 years, which later earned him an honorary doctorate from university president (and future MLB commissioner) Bart Giamatti. And Smoky Joe threw one last pitch at Fenway: before an old-timers' game in 1984, when he was 94 years old.

34

Rob Gronkowski
Patriots Tight End, 2010–2019

Without him, the Deflategate-era Patriots might have collapsed under the weight of their self-righteousness. With him, they could easily have been chop-blocked by silly distractions. Good thing his performance on the field was as over-the-top as his performance off the field.

As it was, the Patriots got the Gronkiest of all worlds: the loosest tight end who ever played. For every eight-catch, 100-yard, two-touchdown tour de force, there was a "Yo soy fiesta" moment of comic relief. At his best, Rob Gronkowski provided both elements at the same time.

Gronkowski's signature game came on a Sunday night at Indianapolis in 2014. On the Gronk scale, his numbers were fairly modest: four catches for 71 yards and a touchdown. But that lone TD was a masterwork. The Pats already led 35–20 with about seven minutes left when Gronkowski caught a short sideline throw from Tom Brady at the Colts 20. Rather than step out of bounds and settle for a first down, Gronk turned upfield. He immediately shed three Colts defenders, outran another to the end zone, and bowled through two others with a flying leap at the goal line. None of the six Indianapolis defenders who had a crack at him looked like they wanted any part of him.

But on his best moment of the night, Gronk was just a blocker. As Jonas Gray walked in for his fourth touchdown, Gronkowski drove Colts defensive back Sergio Brown to the sideline—and then just kept on going, shoving him straight into an NBC camera position. "He was yappin' at me the whole time," Gronk explained later, "so I took him and threw him out of the club."

There was another layer to that story. During a game against the Colts two years earlier, Gronkowski broke his forearm. The player he got locked up with was Sergio Brown.

The most frustrating aspect of that injury was that it occurred as Gronkowski blocked during a meaningless extra-point conversion late in a 59–24 Pats blowout. "I basically only got one speed," he once said. "It's full speed."

The problem is that it's hard to play an entire NFL season at full speed. Already the Pats have seen potential Super Bowl runs derailed in part by Gronk injuries. In that 2012 season he reinjured the arm in a Division Round playoff game against Houston, and in 2013 he tore up his knee in December.

That history, combined with Gronk's full-speed play, often leaves Pats fans holding their breath. It seems absurd—like watching a high-schooler romp through a bunch of pee-wee-leaguers and worrying that *he's* the one who's going to get hurt.

But Pats Nation knows that Gronk's health can mean the difference between winning and losing. With a hurtin' Gronk, the Pats made it to Super Bowl XLVI, but lost to the Giants. With a healthy Gronk, they won Super Bowl XLIX against the Seahawks. In that game he caught six passes for 68 yards, including a 22-yard touchdown, against the NFL's top-rated secondary. He also provided a Gronk-like exclamation point after Malcolm Butler's game-saving interception. When the 'hawks got a little testy during one of Tom Brady's kneel-downs, most of the Patriots opted for restraint, just trying to get off the field.

Not Gronk. "Screw it," he later explained on *Jimmy Kimmel Live*. "Last game of the year, I'm throwin' some haymakers."

Gronkowski helped the Patriots secure another Super Bowl trophy—which he subsequently used as a baseball bat, resulting in a noticeable dent—in a 13–3 win over the Rams before announcing his retirement. If he stays retired, his last catch, good for 29 yards to set up Super Bowl LIII's only touchdown, was a fitting final act.

33

Milt Schmidt
Bruins Center/Defenseman, 1936–1942; 1945–1955

L ike Ted Williams, Milt Schmidt lost some of his prime years to World War II. And in Schmidt's case, those lost years might have had an even greater impact on his team. Unlike Teddy Ballgame, who left a Red Sox team that hadn't sniffed a pennant since World War I, Schmidt's Bruins were at the top of their game. Boston had won the Stanley Cup in 1939 and '41. And the Bruins were still the team to beat on December 9, 1941, when they played the Chicago Blackhawks at the Garden.

It was two days after Pearl Harbor. The game was delayed 45 minutes between periods so the crowd could hear a live broadcast of FDR's Fireside Chat. "We are now in this war," President Roosevelt said. "We are all in it—all the way."

Even though Schmidt, the Bruins center, was from Kitchener, Ontario, he took FDR's words to heart. So did his line mates and fellow Kitcheners, wingers Woody Dumart and Bobby Bauer. Two months later, all three members of the "Kraut Line" left the Bruins for the Royal Canadian Air Force. Some things were more important than hockey. (Leave it to hockey, incidentally, to embrace a politically incorrect nickname like "Kraut Line.")

In their sendoff at the Garden on February 10, 1942, the Kraut Line combined for 22 points as the Bruins thumped Montreal 8–1. Afterward, in a remarkable display of unity, members of both the Bruins and the Canadiens carried the Kraut Line off the ice to a thunderous ovation.

Schmidt didn't suit up for the B's again until the fall of '45. And despite balky knees, he played another nine years in Boston. By the time he retired, he had built a résumé that would land him in the Hall of Fame—including an MVP season in 1950–51.

Even so, the postwar Bruins were unable to regain their championship form. That was in part due to a rule change; the NHL had introduced the red line in 1943 to generate more scoring, which worked against the Bruins' tight-checking prewar approach. For four straight years, from 1937 to '41, they'd had the NHL's best record. Schmidt played his best hockey in those years. He led the NHL in scoring during the 1939–40 season. And although there was no Conn Smythe Trophy in the prewar days, Schmidt probably would have won it in 1941 for his performance during the Bruins' run to the Stanley Cup. After league-leading scorer Bill Cowley went down with a knee injury in the playoff opener, Schmidt picked up the slack. He led all playoff scorers while also putting on what the *Boston Globe*'s Gerry Moore called "one of the greatest exhibitions of body checking by a pivot man in years."

And he provided the pivotal moment in the Final. Up two games to none, the Bruins trailed Game 3 in Detroit, 2-1. A Red Wings win would have made it a series. But back-to-back goals by Schmidt—who was now playing through an injury of his own—put the Bruins ahead to stay. They went on to complete the first four-game sweep in Stanley Cup Final history. And that prompted Moore to declare, "Milton Conrad Schmidt looks more like all the greatest ice stars rolled into one."

Even so, Schmidt and his Kraut Line mates skated away at the pinnacle of their careers, risking not only their livelihood but also their lives—and they did so without hesitation. As Schmidt said years later, "I was very proud of the fact that you were fighting for your country."

After retiring as a player, Schmidt coached the Bruins for most of 11 seasons. Then, as general manager, Schmidt helped assemble the "Big, Bad Bruins" teams that won Stanley Cups in 1970 and '72, giving him a hand in four of the six Bruins championships all time. He died in January 2017, two months shy of his 99th birthday.

32

Jim Rice
Red Sox Outfielder/DH, 1974–1989

He had no signature game, no epic ALCS at-bat, no defining World Series moment. Like Ted Williams, Jim Rice built a Hall of Fame résumé out of chilly April evenings and hot August afternoons, on lots of 2-for-4s and 1-for-3s, on game-tying homers in the fifth inning.

But, also like Williams, Rice had a tantalizing career that invited you to imagine what might have been.

Start with 1975, Rice's first full season. With a .309 average, 22 homers, and 102 RBI, Rice finished second to his "Gold Dust Twins" teammate, Fred Lynn, in Rookie of the Year voting and third in MVP voting. But he broke his hand in September. So he missed that season's classic World Series against Cincinnati's Big Red Machine. With no designated hitter (none was used in the '75 World Series) and no Rice, Sox manager Darrell Johnson put first baseman Carl Yastrzemski in Rice's spot in left and DH Cecil Cooper at first.

The Sox had three one-run losses in that series. Cooper went 1-for-19. Hard not to believe that a young, healthy Jim Ed Rice might have made a difference.

And then there was 1978, Rice's career year. He was named MVP. He led the American League in 11 offensive categories, including those you would expect (46 homers, 139 RBI) and some that you might not (213 hits, 15 triples). And he did it while playing almost every inning of Boston's 163 games.

Game No. 163 was, of course, the AL East tiebreaker at Fenway against the Yankees. Bucky Bleepin' Dent pained all of New England with his pop-fly homer. But Jim Rice probably felt that pain more acutely than anyone else. Had the Red Sox, and not the Yankees, won that game and then the World Series, Rice would have had all the validation he would ever need. But because the Sox lost that tiebreaker (not to mention a 14½-game division lead), the '78 season left a bad aftertaste in Boston—and the sense that Rice's MVP numbers added up to nothing significant.

And then Rice had the temerity to ask for a contract extension that fall. "Jim Rice had a great season and is a great player," wrote the *Globe*'s Larry Whiteside. "He makes a nice impression, if you're looking at the right time. But there are some ugly sides to his personality that he must rid himself of. ... An MVP has to be just that—a Most Valuable Person."

So that's something else Rice and Williams had in common: the enmity of the press. A common presumption was that, as soon as he could, Rice would leave Boston to pursue huge free-agent money elsewhere. But he ended up staying in Boston for his entire career—like Ted Williams.

Rice's excellence became a matter of routine. He led the AL in home runs three times. He had eight seasons with more than 100 RBI. He was an eight-time All-Star.

The last of those All-Star appearances was in 1986, when he hit .324 with 20 homers and 110 RBI. And he finally made it to the postseason.

Everyone knows how *that* story ended. And although Rice acquitted himself fairly well—he had a three-run homer in Game 7 of the Sox' stirring comeback win over the Angels in the ALCS and hit .333 in his only World Series—every player associated with that infamous collapse against the Mets carried an indelible stain. So much so that it took two decades, and the end of an 86-year World Series drought, before the Red Sox got around to retiring Rice's number.

Rice was inducted into the Baseball Hall of Fame in 2009, 15 years after he became eligible. "I wonder why it took so long?" said Rice's former teammate, Carlton Fisk. "When he played, he and Reggie Jackson were the most feared hitters in the league."

31

Ty Law
Patriots Cornerback, 1995–2004

Holy shit! Is this really happening? That was the reaction in living rooms across New England as Ty Law streaked down the Louisiana Superdome sideline in the second quarter of Super Bowl XXXVI.

Sure, this gritty Patriots team had acquitted themselves pretty well so far. They trailed Kurt Warner and the heavily favored St. Louis Rams just 3–0. But the Rams offense was finding a rhythm. After gaining just 22 yards on six carries in the first quarter, running back Marshall Faulk had picked up 20 yards on two straight carries. Would that put the Pats on their heels and allow Warner time to start picking them apart?

Uh, no. On the next play linebacker Mike Vrabel came unblocked on a blitz. Warner's hurried sideline throw to Isaac Bruce was off target. Law, the Pats' veteran cornerback, jumped the route, caught the ball in stride, and ran untouched for a 47-yard pick-six.

Just like that, the Patriots weren't just hanging in there—they were ahead.

It was vintage Ty Law. Throughout his ten years in New England, he had a knack for the big play. He was a four-time pro Bowler whose 36 career interceptions tied Raymond Clayborn's team record. And Law's total included a team-record six pick-sixes.

Law's best all-around performance came in the 2003 AFC Championship Game. He had three difficult interceptions of Colts quarterback Peyton Manning. That was the same number of catches that Manning's favorite receiver, Marvin Harrison, had. "Peyton has confidence in Marvin, and he should," Law said afterward. "But I felt I was up to the challenge. I'm a pretty confident individual also."

Said safety Rodney Harrison, "Ty changed the whole game."

That was true in more ways than one. Law's aggressive play set a tone for the entire New England secondary. Crowding the line of scrimmage, the Pats DBs roughed up the Indy receivers to the point that the Colts later petitioned the league to tighten up the rule on illegal contact.

But law didn't just beat up the Colts' receivers. He also beat them to the ball—and then he had the hands to hold onto it. On his first interception, he laid out and made a fingertip catch on snow-slicked grass. The second was a sliding catch on a Manning overthrow, the third a leaping grab on an underthrow.

The importance of simply catching the ball can't be overstressed. Remember Eli Manning's high throw late in Super Bowl XLII that Asante Samuel had his hands on but couldn't corral? Yes, it would have been a tough catch—but no tougher than the Helmet Catch that David Tyree made on the very next play. Imagine how much better Patriots history would look had Samuel made that pick.

On the other hand, imagine how much worse Pats history would look if Ty Law hadn't held onto that off-target throw from Kurt Warner in Super Bowl XXXVI. That one play not only fired up the Patriots, but it also let the Rams know they were in for a long evening. "I don't think they were up for the fight they were in for," Law said afterward. "We were challenging their guys all game. They're the best track team in the National Football League, but I never seen anyone win a 100-meter dash with somebody standing in front of them."

Law collected a third Super Bowl ring in four years with the Pats after the 2004 season, although he missed the playoffs (and much of the season) with a broken foot. He then left via free agency and recorded a career-high ten interceptions with the Jets in 2005. He also played with the Chiefs and Broncos before retiring after the '09 season. He was inducted into the Patriots Hall of Fame in 2014, his first year of eligibility.

30

Jason Varitek
Red Sox Catcher, 1997–2011

I n his autobiography, Pedro Martinez listed four reasons why he became baseball's most dominant pitcher in 1999 and 2000. Reason No. 4? "Jason Varitek became my catcher."

That's a pretty solid endorsement for a guy who was considered a bonus in an addition-by-subtraction deadline deal. In 1997, Sox GM Dan Duquette shipped disastrous closer Heathcliff Slocumb (0-5, 5.79 ERA, five blown saves in 22 tries) to the Seattle Mariners for Varitek and pitcher Derek Lowe, a pair of minor league prospects. It proved to be one of the great heists in major league history.

When first told of the deal, Varitek gave Sox fans a taste of the attitude that he'd be packing on the plane ride from Triple-A Tacoma. "I'm real happy," he said. "It doesn't get much better than the Red Sox tradition. Now I've got to get there and get ready."

Those who delved deeper found that the young catcher had solid credentials. Varitek was Baseball America's 1993 College Player of the Year and a former MVP of the Cape Cod League. But what was most striking about Varitek's background was not the individual honors he'd accumulated. It was his history of playing on winning teams, at every level. He'd played in the Little League World Series. His Florida high school team (nicknamed the Patriots, incidentally) won a state championship. His college team, Georgia Tech, made it to the title game of the 1994 College World Series.

So the evidence of what Jason Varitek brought to Boston was already there in August 1997. He was a hardworking baseball traditionalist who instilled a winning attitude everywhere he went.

It took a while, but all of those traits eventually surfaced at the major league level. Varitek ended up catching 1,488 games for the Sox, most in team history. Along the way he added enough offense to become an All-Star, with three seasons with 20 or more home runs. But he made his primary contribution behind the plate. "He studies the opposing hitters to such a degree, and fits this knowledge with the particular abilities of the pitchers, that his signal-calling is amazing," said Curt Schilling. "It seems that every time I shake him off, something bad happens."

Schilling and Pedro, of course, would have looked good with any catcher. It's what Varitek did with the rest of the staff that stood out. He caught four no-hitters, most in major league history. Look at who threw them: Hideo Nomo, Derek Lowe, Clay Buchholz, and Jon Lester.

Varitek was such an acknowledged leader that he became just the third player in the Red Sox' long history to be named captain. He was rarely outspoken in public, preferring to handle team matters in-house. Still, a national TV audience saw evidence of his fire on July 24, 2004. Varitek stuffed his mitt in Alex Rodriguez's face after the Yankees prima donna complained about being beaned with a Bronson Arroyo *breaking ball*. That triggered a brawl that fueled a Boston comeback. The Red Sox rallied from five runs down to beat the Yankees. Varitek was long gone by the end, ejected for force-feeding A-Rod some leather. But he was behind the plate three months later at Yankee Stadium, when the Red Sox completed a comeback of far greater magnitude, coming from 3–0 down to win the ALCS, en route to ending an 86-year World Series dry spell.

Said Schilling when it was over, "Ladies and gentlemen, here is the leader of the 2004 Boston Red Sox."

He was talking about Jason Varitek, whose knack for turning teams into winners had passed the ultimate test.

Three years later Varitek led a much different staff, one that included Josh Beckett and Japanese import Daisuke Matsuzaka, to another World Series title.

29

John Hannah
Patriots Left Guard, 1973–1985

It's fitting that the first Patriots player inducted into the Pro Football Hall of Fame was an offensive lineman. During the team's first quarter-century there was little dazzle. Two division titles. One Super Bowl appearance (a crushing defeat). One season of All-Pro quarterback play, back in the days when the American Football League had just eight teams. Stranded on the margins of Boston sports, Pats fans had to grasp whatever dignity they could find

Fortunately, they had John Hannah to rally around.

Hannah, a left guard for life, was a 6'2" 270-pound son of the South. He was what they used to call "country strong." He played 13 seasons in Foxboro, from 1973 through 1985, and made the Pro Bowl nine times. It would have been ten if he and linemate Leon Gray hadn't held out for the first three games of the 1977 season. Hannah: "Bad little boys in the NFL don't get picked to the Pro Bowl."

No one pushed John Hannah around. Not opposing linemen and not the guy who signed his checks.

Hannah's 33-inch thighs gave him an immovable foundation. He combined that with quickness, honed through years of wrestling, and startling foot speed. "We were all shocked," said Ron Erhardt, who was the Pats backfield coach during Hannah's first mini-camp. "That's all we talked about that night, this big guy coming down the runway and, bang, hitting the clock in 4.8."

Football junkies loved him. Once, when asked to name the one player he would choose to build a franchise around, John Madden picked Hannah. In a 1981 *Sports Illustrated* article, esteemed football writer Paul Zimmerman, aka "Dr. Z," named Hannah the best offensive lineman of all time. His cover story included this assessment from Bucko Kilroy, who was the Pats director of player personnel when they drafted Hannah out of Alabama: "For all his size and explosiveness and straight-ahead speed, John has something none of the other [great linemen] ever had, and that's phenomenal, repeat, *phenomenal* lateral agility and balance—the same as defensive backs."

Hannah was the lynchpin on the 1978 Patriots line that cleared the way for a 3,165-yard rushing season, which remains the best in NFL history.

That season Hannah also had what he once called his signature game, in Dallas against the defending Super Bowl champion Cowboys. Hannah went head to head with defensive tackle Randy White, another future Hall of Famer, who matched Hannah Pro Bowl for Pro Bowl. "John Hannah—he's everything people say," White said afterward. "He was trying to kick my ass and I was trying to kick his."

Hannah got the better of it, particularly when he pancaked White to spring Sam Cunningham for a 52-yard touchdown run. But while Hannah won that battle, the Cowboys won the war. Dallas beat New England 17–10, largely because Pats kicker Dave Posey had two field goal attempts blocked and hooked another from 39 yards.

That game summarized Hannah's career. He performed at an elite level against the best in the business—but the rest of the team couldn't match his talent or his effort.

When John Hannah finally made it to the Super Bowl, he was almost 35 years old, playing with two shredded rotator cuffs and a powdered left knee. And he had to go against the '85 Bears, a team that stands as one of the best ever. The results were ugly—a 46–10 Chicago rout. "Play after play as I crashed into the Bears defensive line my knee became blazing white hot with agonizing pain," Hannah later wrote in his autobiography. He knew the end had come. "I most assuredly was not going to risk all those years being called 'the best' only to be replaced involuntarily because I couldn't cut it anymore." So he retired. Five years later, in his first appearance on the ballot, he was in the Pro Football Hall of Fame. As he and his father, Herb—another southern farm boy who'd played in the NFL—were leaving for the ceremony, John accidentally stepped in a pile of horseshit. Herb told him that was a sign "not to forget your roots."

28

Cam Neely
Bruins Right Winger, 1986–1996

He never won a Stanley Cup, but it was not from lack of effort. Cam Neely is the Bruins' all-time leader in playoff goals (55), including 11 game-winners, another franchise record.

But it was more than just his clutch scoring that set Neely apart. In an organization renowned for tough guys, Neely might have been the toughest of all. It wasn't just the way he used his size (6'1", 218 pounds) to dish out big hits. Nor was it his willingness to drop the gloves (in the 1988–89 season he served more than three hours in the penalty box). Said former Bruin Terry O'Reilly, a pretty tough guy himself, "He fought, he shot, and he checked, and it was utterly impossible to stop him."

But what truly distinguished Cam Neely was the way he fought through injuries. Some were relatively minor. He once received 16 stitches in his forehead during a game—and promptly tore them open in a fight. Another time he returned to the ice after having a nearly-severed fingertip reattached. And the only reason he even missed a shift was that "it just took some time for the doc to get there.")

But he also dealt with more major injuries than any one player should have to endure.

Neely's ordeal started with a knee injury during a May 1991 playoff game, when the Penguins' Ulf Samuelsson threw a leg check. Neely played through that injury and finished the series. In the final game, attempting payback, Neely inadvertently slammed his left thigh into Samuelsson's knee. The result was a deep bruise that slowly hardened into a solid mass. Bruins fans learned a new term: *myositis ossificans.*

Neely says he heard some grim prognoses during the offseason—"everything from 'career-ending' to … 'amputation.' "

He didn't return to the ice until January 1992. After scoring nine goals in nine games, Neely was sidelined again with a left knee injury that he initially said "doesn't look too serious." He thought he would be back in February. And he was—February of *1993*. In the interim he had two rounds of surgery to remove damaged cartilage.

After 13 months on the shelf, he scored within his first five minutes back in action. It was an electrifying Garden moment, but also a bittersweet one. Still just 27 years old, Cam Neely had lost almost two full seasons of his hockey prime.

He never did return to full strength, but his resolve and his skills were undiminished. To reduce the strain on his knee, Neely limited his starts the following season. The result was unlike anything the NHL had ever seen. Neely played like an MVP one night and took a DNP the next. He ended up with the third 50-goal season of his career—and he netted No. 50 in just his 44th game. Only Wayne Gretzky had done it in fewer.

But Neely's season ended after just his 49th game, when he tore the MCL in his other knee. Again he rehabbed, again he came back, and again he showed flashes of brilliance (he led the league in power-play goals during the lockout-shortened season the following year). But in 1996, when Neely was still just 31, an injury to his right hip ended a career that was as frustrating as it was brilliant. "If I've got a regret," Neely said, "it's just that I wish I could have retired on my own terms."

Neely had his No. 8 retired to the Garden rafters in 2004 and was inducted into the Hockey Hall of Fame in 2005. And in his current role as Bruins president, Neely finally got to celebrate a Stanley Cup in 2011. After Boston missed the playoffs for the second straight year in 2016, however, some Bruins fans began saying what would once have been unthinkable: Maybe it's time for the team to cut Cam loose.

27

Sam Jones
Celtics Guard, 1957–1969

Not every Hall of Fame-caliber shooting guard would have been content to come off the bench. But that was never an issue for Sam Jones, who won ten NBA championships in his 12-year career with the Celtics. In fact, Jones was bothered more by that "Hall of Fame" designation than by his role as a role player. "I put team before individuals," he said at his 1984 induction ceremony in Springfield. "There are 26 other Celtics who are not here who made it possible for me to be here."

He then name-checked most of them, giving shout-outs to Jungle Jim Loscutoff and Lou Tsioropoulos, Wayne Embry and Em Bryant, Willie Naulls and Clyde Lovelette—even Johnny McCarthy, an obscure point guard who played in just 28 games for the Celtics.

But while those members of the Celtics' supporting cast made important contributions, the most critical skill on any team is the ability to put the ball in the basket, particularly under duress. And few players have done that better over an extended period than Sam Jones. In big games he produced both quantity scoring (47 points in a Game 7 win over the Cincinnati Royals in the 1963 Eastern Division Finals) and quality scoring (game-winning buckets against the Sixers in Game 7 of the 1962 Eastern Division Finals, and against the Lakers in Game 4 of the 1969 NBA Finals).

For five straight years he led the Celtics in scoring during the regular season. For three straight championship seasons he led them in playoff scoring. His 51 points against the Pistons in October 1965 stood as Boston's regular-season record until Larry Bird broke it with a 53-point game in 1983. (Jones also set a Celtics playoff-game record with a 51-point game against the Knicks in 1967; John Havlicek broke it with a 54-point game in 1973.)

With his quickness and his ability to use the backboard from a variety of angles, Sam Jones could score with the best of them. And yet, even as he became the prime crunch-time option on the top NBA dynasty ever, he maintained his humility. Maybe that's because he arrived from obscurity. Red Auerbach chose him, sight unseen, from tiny North Carolina College (now called North Carolina Central), with the Celtics' first pick in the 1957 NBA Draft. (Wake Forest coach Bones McKinney recommended him.)

Maybe it's because he joined a team that already had *three* future Hall of Famers (Bob Cousy, Bill Sharman, and Frank Ramsey) in the backcourt. "When I first reported to the Boston Celtics, I thought it would be for just a few days," Jones said during his twelfth and final season. It wasn't until 1961 that Jones cracked the starting lineup, through injuries and attrition.

Whatever the reason, Jones had an unselfish approach—a characteristic that Auerbach had an uncanny ability to sniff out. He was also fundamentally sound (he hit 80.3% of his free throws during his career), another hallmark of those great '60s Celtics teams.

Bill Russell and he were the only two Celtics along for that entire ride in the 1960s. (Russell, who was drafted a year before Jones, won 11 titles in 13 years.) And they were the perfect complementary pieces: a dominant defender and rebounder in the post and a slick-shooting guard in the backcourt.

But again, Jones would be the first to remind you that they had plenty of help. "It wasn't only about Bill Russell or Sam Jones," he said in a 2007 interview with Celtic Nation's Michael D. McCllellan. "It was about the entire team, the roles we played, and the sacrifices that we made in order to achieve something bigger."

Although Jones was reluctant to boast of his individual accomplishments, his résumé did it for him. In 1996, during the league's 50th anniversary celebration, he was named one of the NBA's 50 Greatest Players. And at a Boston Garden ceremony in March 1969 honoring Jones on the verge of his retirement, Auerbach paid the ultimate compliment. Said Red, "I would like to thank Sam Jones for making me a helluva coach."

26

Tedy Bruschi
Patriots Linebacker, 1996–2008

One Pro Bowl? Seriously? Tedy Bruschi played in just *one* Pro Bowl? When the Patriots won three Super Bowls in four years, largely on the strength of a stifling defense, it seemed like No. 54 was always in the center of things, both on the field and in the locker room. (*Awwwww-yeah!*)

"It's impossible to put value on everything the guy does," fellow linebacker Mike Vrabel once told *Sports Illustrated*.

Like Vrabel (just one Pro Bowl for him, too), Bruschi was undervalued around the league. But he was highly valued in New England— for his toughness, his leadership, and his adaptability (he'd been a defensive end in college). And, like Vrabel, he had an uncanny ability as a playmaker. "It seems like every time I get the ball I have a chance to score," Bruschi said one time.

During a stretch of the 2002 and '03 seasons, Bruschi converted four straight interceptions into touchdowns. His most celebrated pick-six came in a December 2003 game at Foxboro. Conditions were eerily similar to the infamous "Snow Plow Game" of 1982. Same heavy dose of the white stuff, same opponent—the Miami Dolphins. And for the longest time the Pats held the same precarious lead: 3–0. But with nine minutes left, Dolphins quarterback Jay Fiedler fired a quick slant over the middle from his own end zone. Bruschi snatched it at the line of scrimmage and skated five yards into the end zone, where he slid across the snowy turf on his knees.

The runback might have been easy, but the interception wasn't. Playing in numbing New England cold, the California native and

University of Arizona grad picked off a bullet pass from point-blank range. "Tedy's play there was one of the all-time greatest individual plays I've ever seen," said Pats special-teams wizard Larry Izzo.

The pick-six sealed both the game and the AFC East title. As Gary Glitter's "Rock n Roll Part II" blared, Pats fans around Gillette Stadium threw handfuls of snow in the air in time with the "Hey!" chant. It looked like thousands of confetti canons going off at once.

This was a unique time in Pats history, a run that produced both a 21-game winning streak and back-to-back Super Bowl wins ('03 and '04). And Bruschi was an essential cog. He had his two highest tackle totals in those seasons, including 5½ sacks, along with his knack for timely turnovers. He was named AFC Defensive Player of the Week after the Patriots' 20–3 win over Peyton Manning and the Colts in a 2004 division-round game, when he was credited with two fumble recoveries. One was a literal takeaway; Bruschi simply ripped the ball out of running back Dominic Rhodes' hands.

After that 2004 season Bruschi made his lone Pro Bowl appearance. Just three days later he suffered a stroke, traced to a congenital heart defect. And while he was quickly diagnosed and treated—he was at Fenway on Opening Day to honor the Red Sox for their historic World Series run the previous fall—he announced that he would sit out the 2005 season. "I think I've healed faster physically than I have emotionally," he said.

But when the season began and the Patriots' defense struggled, Bruschi's emotions slipped back into competitive mode. Six weeks in, the two-defending Super Bowl champs were 3–3 and had forced just one turnover. They needed their playmaker back. So, on a Sunday night at the end of October, Bruschi returned. After the game, when the Pats had secured a 21–16 victory over Buffalo, it was coach Bill Belichick who led the team cheer instead of No. 54. Said Belichick, "I wanna know how we feel about having Tedy Bruschi back?"

Awwww-yeah!

Bruschi played another 3½ seasons before announcing his retirement— which he did in true Patriots style. "When you come into this facility there is a sign," Bruschi said. "Bill does a great job of always emphasizing this. 'Do your job.' Well, I did my job for 13 years and now my job is done."

25

Carlton Fisk
Red Sox Catcher, 1969; 1971–1980

He created an oasis. Beyond, the desert stretched to the horizon in all directions. Season after season, for most of a century, the Boston Red Sox were generally either downright terrible or a terrible tease.

And in a warped way, Carlton Fisk provided the cruelest tease of all.

Thanks to Pudge, sleep-deprived Sox fans spent one glorious, giddy October day stoned on a cocktail of relief and belief. Boston had advanced from the brink of elimination—down three games to two in the 1975 World Series against Cincinnati's Big Red Machine—to one game of winner-take-all, right there at Fenway Park.

And the decisive blow, a twelfth-inning walk-off home run off the Reds' Pat Darcy, and off the leftfield foul pole, the most clutch Sox hit in history to that point, had been struck by a fellow member of Red Sox Nation. As he hopped to first, he frantically waved the ball fair—a proxy for all those jangled Sox fans from Bridgeport to Fort Kent.

Carlton Fisk, whose hometown name-checked half the New England states: Charlestown, New Hampshire, right across the Connecticut River from Vermont. Carlton Fisk, the 1972 AL Rookie of the Year—first to win that award unanimously. Carlton Fisk, the strong, ornery, take-no-crap catcher who had almost singlehandedly rekindled the long-dormant rivalry with the Yankees. (He and Thurman Munson intensified their one-on-one battle to become the AL's dominant catcher with a brawl in the summer of '73.) Carlton Fisk, who fought back from injuries with the same intensity that he displayed when fighting Sox opponents.

Rehabbing first from a torn-up knee and then a broken forearm, Fisk missed a year between June of '74 and June of '75. But he bounced back and hit .331, a career high, over the second half of that '75 season before blasting what still stands as the most famous World Series home run in Sox history—the one that set Fenway fans up to celebrate Boston baseball's first title since 1918.

But of course it didn't work out that way.

That '75 World Series summed up Carlton Fisk's time with the Red Sox. He did his part to try to bring a World Series to Boston—but the Red Sox couldn't close the deal. Happened again in '78. Fisk played through a broken rib and a bothersome elbow—and played well enough to make the All-Star team for the sixth time in seven years, all while setting an American League record for games caught in a single season. But the Sox couldn't hold a 14½-game lead in the AL East.

His time in Boston ended because the Red Sox literally couldn't close the deal. After the 1980 season, Sox GM Haywood Sullivan mailed Fisk's contract a day after the renewal deadline. That made Fisk a free agent, and he used that freedom to change his Sox from Red to White.

He ended up playing in Chicago for 13 seasons. He made two more All-Star teams: in 1985, when he had career highs in home runs (37) and RBI (107) and in 1991. By then he was 43 years old and playing in his fourth decade of Major League Baseball.

In June 1993, just before he retired, Fisk set a major league record for games caught in a career (since surpassed). And although the record-setting game was in Chicago, Fisk hired a plane to fly over Fenway bearing a banner that read: "It all started here. Thanks, Boston fans. Pudge Fisk."

A big question in the run-up to Fisk's Hall of Fame induction in 2000 was which Sox hat he would wear at the ceremony. He picked the red one, of course. "I grew up in New Hampshire and my roots are in New England," he explained. "When I grew up, my dream was to be the starting power forward for the Boston Celtics. But my second choice was to wear a Boston Red Sox uniform."

24

Andre Tippett
Patriots Linebacker, 1982–1993

During the mid-'80s Pats fans could count on three things each year. The Patriots would be good enough to raise hopes but flawed enough to dash them. There would be a quarterback controversy. And Andre Tippett would make the Pro Bowl.

For five years, from 1984 through '88, Tippet was both the best linebacker in the AFC and the best linebacker the Patriots have ever had. His 18.5 sacks in 1984 still stands as the franchise record. His 35 sacks in '84 and '85 is the highest two-year total for any linebacker in NFL history. "Tippett's definitely the catalyst of the [New England] defense," said Jets quarterback Pat Ryan. "He's like a great defensive end playing linebacker."

Said Bills quarterback Jim Kelly, "You have to change your style of offense to compensate for his ability to rush the passer."

But Tippett wasn't merely a pass-rush specialist. "That guy is simply just a great football player," said Dolphins coach Don Shula. "You have to respect him every down."

When the Patriots squished Shula's fish in the 1985 AFC Championship game 31–14, ending a 20-year losing streak in Miami, Tippett was one of the primary reasons why. He was the unquestioned leader of a hardnosed defense that knocked the fight—and everything else—out of the Dolphins. "You have to give New England credit," Miami quarterback Dan Marino said. "They don't get fancy. They are just tough. They just play simple, basic football, but they are a physical team."

Tippett set the tone. Along with his 16.5 sacks in 1985, he also had four fumble recoveries. But his biggest achievement of that Super Bowl season might have come in the locker room. When a 24–20 loss to a mediocre Browns team dropped the Patriots to 2–3, Tippett went off on his teammates. The simple message behind his tirade: Stop making excuses. "He told us pretty plainly that it was about time we accepted the responsibility for winning," said running back Tony Collins.

The '85 Patriots took Tippett's message to heart. From that point on the team went 9–2 to land a wild card berth. Tippett was immense, winning AFC Defensive Player of the Year honors. He logged five multi-sack games, the most impressive of which was a three-sack performance against the Jets in which he fought through repeated double teams. Said Tippett, "I just made up my mind I was going to get back there no matter how many people they were going to put on me."

When the Patriots faced the Jets again in the wild-card round of the '85 playoffs, Tippett had just one sack, but it was huge. He knocked out starting quarterback Ken O'Brien in the second quarter. ("That would have knocked out Muhammad Ali," said backup quarterback Pat Ryan.) The Pats went on to win 26–14, their first playoff victory in 22 years.

It's unfortunate that the '85 Patriots season ended with a crushing Super Bowl loss to the Bears, and that Tippett never enjoyed another playoff victory. Had his team accomplished more, Tippett would have received the individual recognition he deserved. "I've always thought the guys who played on losing teams in their career get short shrift in Hall of Fame consideration," said *Sports Illustrated*'s Peter King, "and [Tippett] is a classic example. He was the primary focus of the opposing game plan. To have been consistently outstanding for a decade, and to have averaged ten sacks a year with what he faced every week, is worthy of my Hall vote."

Although he retired as a player in 1993 (with 100 career sacks), Tippett has remained a member of the Patriots organization ever since (he's currently the team's executive director of community affairs). And in 2008, ten years after he became eligible, he finally made the Pro Football Hall of Fame. "I am so proud to be a Patriot for 26 years," he said during his induction speech in Canton, "and I hope to be a Patriot for another 26 years."

23

Roger Clemens
Red Sox Pitcher, 1984–1996

Older Red Sox fans look at his career through bifocals. From a certain angle they can still see the prime Rocket years in HD. From 1986 through 1992, Roger Clemens was baseball's best pitcher. He won three Cy Young Awards in seven seasons. His record over that stretch: 136–63, 2.66 ERA, 81 complete games (including 33 shutouts), and an average of 239 strikeouts per season.

Most telling of all, the Red Sox made the postseason three times in five years, the first time they had done that since World War I.

Clemens made the Red Sox matter again. When he set Boston abuzz on April 29, 1986, by striking out 20 Seattle Mariners, just 13,414 fans were in Fenway Park to see it. Average attendance at his remaining 13 Fenway starts that season was 30,331. Clemens became appointment viewing, the first Sox pitcher to achieve that since Luis Tiant in 1972.

Just as compelling as the substance of a Clemens performance was the style. Unlike so many other Sox starters, who seemed to shrink in the shadow of the Green Monster, Clemens stood tall. He pitched inside, threw Texas heat, and stared batters down. "You're not talking about a normal pitcher when you talk about Clemens," said Baltimore Orioles HOF-pitcher-turned broadcaster Jim Palmer. "He's different."

If he wasn't quite in a class by himself, he kept exclusive company: Clemens won 192 games during his time in Boston, tying him with Cy Young for the all-time team lead.

And that's why so many Sox fans took such a dim view of what came later.

Older fans revered the Rocket so much, most even took his side when he left via free agency in the fall of '96. They blamed GM Dan Duquette for letting Clemens walk to Toronto. Duquette's lame rationalization: "Roger hasn't won a Cy Young in a while."

Well, Clemens remedied that, winning back-to-back Cy Young Awards during his two years in Toronto. And when he marched into Fenway for the first time wearing enemy colors in July of '97, he walked off the field to a standing O and chants of *Rock-et, Rock-et!* He'd set a Toronto record with 16 strikeouts in a 4–1 Blue Jays win—the last three Ks coming on just ten pitches against the top of the Sox order.

But everything changed in February of '99. When Clemens joined a Yankees team that had just won the World Series with a 125–50 record, he became—in Boston's eyes—a soulless mercenary. He was no longer the leader he had once seemed—he was a contemptible bandwagon-hopper. New York was simply the path of least resistance to a World Series ring. *If you can't beat the Yankees,* Clemens declared with his actions, *join 'em.*

That was a deal no true Red Sox fan could ever endorse.

The Yankee deal was far from the last of the ill feelings Sox fans developed for Clemens. Throw in the Mitchell Report, the bizarre episodes with Mike Piazza, the serial retirement announcements, and a seemingly endless series of logic-challenging quotes, and it became impossible for a huge segment of Red Sox Nation to forgive Roger Clemens, even if they never forgot that he was the best homegrown pitcher they ever saw.

22

Terry O'Reilly
Bruins Right Winger, 1972–1985

Today the incident sounds so politically incorrect that it could be part of Louis CK's "Of course … but maybe" bit.

Of course no hockey player should ever go into the stands and put his hands on a fan. Of course he shouldn't. Of course. … But maybe if the fan is dumb enough to steal a player's stick and try to hit him with it, he deserves to get the shit kicked out of him.

It was December 1979. The Bruins had just held on for a tense 4–3 win over the Rangers at Madison Square Garden. Players lingered on the ice, jawing and pushing. Not unusual for the NHL—certainly not in the '70s. But then a Rangers fan leaned over the boards and sucker-punched Bruins left wing Stan Jonathan, who had scored the winning goal. Jonathan, whose nose was bloodied, raised his stick in self-defense. The fan pulled it away and brandished it like a weapon.

Bruins' right winger Terry O'Reilly immediately clambered over the boards and disarmed the stick-swinger with what he called "sort of a bear hug." Eight other Bruins followed O'Reilly into the stands and mixed it up with a handful of other fans. The brawl lasted a few minutes before security—aided by Bruins coach Fred Creighton and GM Harry Sinden—got things under control. There were no serious injuries, and as far as the Bruins were concerned, no reason to feel contrite. As The *Boston Globe*'s Francis Rosa reported, "Out of [the fight] came a team unity, a soaring morale."

NHL president John Ziegler didn't see the Bruins as heroes in a morality play. He slapped O'Reilly with an eight-game suspension.

O'Reilly was furious. "I question his competence," he said of Ziegler. But it's unlikely that O'Reilly would have changed a thing, even knowing what the outcome would be. No Bruin was ever more protective of his teammates. For 13 years O'Reilly patrolled the ice at Boston Garden, keeping a watchful eye on a succession of scorers that ranged from Bobby Orr and Phil Esposito to Raymond Bourque and Rick Middleton.

But although O'Reilly ended up the Bruins all-time leader in penalty minutes and used to poke fun at his limited skating ability, he wasn't a goon. He wasn't even an "enforcer" per se. He was a respectable winger—a two-time All-Star with a knack for timely scoring, particularly when teamed with center Peter McNab. O'Reilly once put up 90 points in a season, and had a career plus/minus of +212.

And it was his power-play goal that had sparked a three-goal third period that pushed the Bruins past the Rangers on the night of the infamous Madison Square Garden brawl.

No wonder New York fans were in such a testy mood. Still, provoking the Big, Bad Bruins was crazy—as that hapless fan must have realized when he found himself suffering the wrath of O'Reilly. Said O'Reilly, "Are you getting your money's worth?"

It was only fair. With a drive that far exceeded his ability, Terry O'Reilly always gave Bruins fans *their* money's worth.

O'Reilly served as the Bruins captain for the final two seasons of his playing career. He then coached for three seasons, leading the Bruins to the Stanley Cup Final in 1988 (and ending a 45-year playoff drought against Montreal in the process). He resigned the following year, in part so he could spend more time with his son Evan, who was seriously ill with liver disease. The Bruins retired his number, 24, to the rafters in 2002— an honor his former teammate, Mike Milbury, said he was absolutely entitled to, despite his lack of a Hall of Fame résumé. "Terry O'Reilly was an old-time Bruin, an old-time warrior," Milbury said. "He deserves to be up where those other guys are."

21

Paul Pierce
Celtics Small Forward/Shooting Guard, 1998–2013

Long before he played with Kevin Garnett he played with Marlon Garnett, among many other forgettable Celtics. (Remember J.R. Bremer?) He endured Rick Pitino. His missed the postseason five times in his first nine years. He suffered through terrible lows. Some occurred off the court (he was stabbed multiple times at the Buzz Club in September 2000). Many more happened on the court (the lowest point was when he was ejected late in a tight 2005 playoff game after throwing an elbow following a hard foul by the Pacers' Jamaal Tinsley, an act that hoops god Bob Ryan called "the single most unforgivable, untimely, stupid, and flat-out selfish on-court act in the history of the Celtics").

But Paul Pierce stuck with Boston and Boston stuck with him. And in the span of one remarkable year, he went from slogging through an injury-shortened season on a last-place team to celebrating as MVP of the 2008 NBA Finals.

That changed everything. "I'm not living under the shadows of the other greats now," Pierce said afterward. "If I was going to be [among] the best Celtics to ever play, I had to put up a banner. And today we did that."

He played five more years in Boston. And one by one he passed most of those Celtics greats in the record book. No Celtic made more free throws or drilled more three-pointers, an indication of Pierce's all-around offensive game. Only John Havlicek scored more points for the C's. Only Larry Bird had a higher career scoring average. No. 34

has earned a place alongside No. 17 and No. 33 in the rafters at the new Garden.

But it wasn't Pierce's individual numbers that branded him one of the Celtics' all-time great gamers. It was his commitment to winning a championship as part of a team. When Danny Ainge arranged to bring in Kevin Garnett and Ray Allen in the summer of 2007, Pierce didn't fret about how many shots he would get. Instead, the Celtics captain said, "This is a dream come true. I feel like a rookie again."

And he performed like it, slimming down to his college playing weight of around 230. "I'm focusing on my defense, being able to guard all three positions," Pierce said. "The stuff I think about is if I have to go to shooting guard and defend and take pressure off Ray. I just want the footwork and quickness."

In other words, Paul Pierce focused on the same thing in 2007 that Red Auerbach had in 1957. Championship basketball started with hard work and team defense.

After beating his hometown team, the LA Lakers, in the 2008 NBA Finals, Pierce came up just short in a 2010 rematch. Three years later, the new "Big Three" era ended as it had begun, with a blockbuster mid-summer trade. Ainge dealt Pierce and Garnett (along with Jason Terry and D.J. White) to the Brooklyn Nets. Ainge expressed gratitude along with regret, saying in a statement, "We would not have won banner 17 without Paul and Kevin and they will go down amongst the all-time great players to have ever worn a Celtics uniform." Pierce ended his career with the Clippers in 2017, sinking the last shot he ever took at the Garden on Super Bowl Sunday, a few hours before the Pats stunned the Falcons.

20

John L. Sullivan
World Heavyweight Boxing Champion, 1882–1892

He fought the law and *he* won. Southie's John L. Sullivan became the first athlete to earn $1 million in his career, and he did it through prizefighting, a sport that was illegal when he started. As a teenager in the 1870s Sullivan would go to various Boston bars and offer to fight any man in the place for a price.

Most states, including Massachusetts, had already outlawed the bare-knuckle bouts that had been popular earlier in the century. Eventually, some boxing promoters figured out that they could circumvent the law by adopting the so-called "Queensberry Rules," which required the boxers to wear gloves. Promoters also advertised their bouts as "exhibitions," in which the boxers would simply demonstrate their skills, sort of like fencing.

The only skill Sullivan cared to exhibit was his awesome punching power. Take his bout at Boston Music Hall on April 6, 1880. His opponent was Englishman Joe Goss, who was recognized as heavyweight champion. Some who knew Sullivan feared that his unsophisticated approach wouldn't fly against an experienced pugilist.

They immediately learned otherwise. Wrote the *Boston Globe*, "The first round was a surprise to the friends of the young Bostonian, who with more skill than was expected planted blow after blow with his left on the face of the champion."

The second round brought more of the same, with Sullivan "getting in no less than four sledge-hammer-like blows upon the right ear of Goss, and the latter went reeling to the floor. … The affair, on the whole, was one of the most interesting and exciting of its kind that ever was witnessed in this city."

Sullivan's popularity soon spread nationwide. He toured the country, giving exhibitions in which he would destroy some poor local pug, often in the first round, at venues ranging from shadowy saloons to roller rinks to opera houses to, in one famous early episode, a barge in the Hudson River. As often as not it was the police, not the referee, who stopped the fights. Operating on the threshold of lawlessness only added to Sullivan's appeal.

The bout that cemented the Sullivan legend occurred on July 8, 1889, in the wilds of Mississippi. Sullivan was still undefeated, but had begun to show signs of fallibility due to age, a bout of serious illness, and what one paper termed "a course of drinking and dissipation." A new challenger, Jake Kilrain, had recently fought to a draw in France against English champion Jem Smith in an epic 106-round duel. Kilrain thought he could whip Sullivan in a battle of attrition. So he issued a challenge to the Boston Strong Boy.

The build-up lasted months and drew enormous interest in the press. The details were hammered out six months in advance: It would be an old-fashioned bare-knuckle bout, for a purse of $20,000, plus the Richard K. Fox belt (named for a millionaire sportsman and "understood to be emblematic of the fistic championship of America"). But the location was described only as "within 200 miles of New Orleans," owing to the fight's murky legal status.

The fact that both Louisiana governor Francis T. Nicholls and Mississippi governor Robert Lowry vowed to prevent the bout added to the intrigue. A man named Charley Rich arranged to hold the fight on his property near a Mississippi farm, in a temporary outdoor ring. And somehow he managed to transport 3,000 Gilded Age A-listers, along with members of the press, by train to the "secret" location. (As the *Boston Globe* noted, "All of Gov. Lowry's attempts to stop the fight seem to have been remarkably unfortunate.")

The bout was supposed to start at daybreak, but it was after ten a.m. by the time all the spectators arrived—some perched atop the railroad cars. By then the temperature was already pushing 100 degrees. But other than a surprise knockdown in the first round, and a spell of vomiting in the 44th (which he attributed to sour lemon in his between-rounds iced tea; others said the tea was spiked with whisky), Sullivan dominated the fight. At one point he taunted Kilrain, asking, "You are a champion? A champion of what?"

The fight lasted two hours and 15 minutes. By one unofficial estimate, Sullivan won 68 of 75 rounds. He had also trained outdoors and had a tan. The pallid Kilrain suffered a severe sunburn, among his many other injuries. The fight was scheduled for 80 rounds, but after round 75 a doctor warned Kilrain's corner that their man might die if the fight continued. So they "tossed in the sponge," ending America's last high-profile bare-knuckle fight.

Although others may have doubted Sullivan at that stage, he did not. "Of course I won," he said afterward. "I expected that."

Wrote the *Globe*, "John L. Sullivan is still the bright particular star of the pugilistic firmament."

Sullivan's only official loss occurred on September 7, 1892 at the Olympic Club in New Orleans, against Gentleman Jim Corbett—a refined, college-educated boxer who likely never would have gone into the fight game if Sullivan hadn't made it so popular. Sullivan, who died on February 2, 1918, was among the inaugural class inducted into the International Boxing Hall of Fame in 1990.

19

Johnny Bucyk
Bruins Left Winger, 1957–1978

Like another famous No. 9, he seemed destined to end his distinguished career in Boston without reaching his ultimate goal: winning a championship. Johnny Bucyk had come to the Bruins in 1957, traded from Detroit for legendary goalie Terry Sawchuk. That year he helped carry a mediocre team to the Stanley Cup Final before losing to Montreal. And then the roof caved in.

Bucyk continued to play at a high level for the next decade. As the Chief on the "Uke Line" (along with fellow Ukrainian–Canadians Bronco Horvath and Vic Stasiuk), Bucyk led the Bruins in scoring four times. But not one of those teams even made the playoffs.

Still, Bucyk showed up and played night after night. During one three-year stretch he missed just three games. And it's not as if he shied away from contact. He had a knack for devastating, though clean, hip checks.

By the spring of 1968 Bucyk had become the Bruins' all-time leader in both goals and total points. But the 32-year-old winger was also playing in a back brace because of a degenerative disc. So when the Bruins held John Bucyk Night that March, it felt like a farewell.

He ended up playing another ten years.

Although Bucyk enjoyed a renaissance as the senior member of the Big, Bad Bruins that won the Stanley Cup in 1970 and '72, he was wise enough to recognize whose team it was. "When Bobby [Orr] came to his first camp, they asked if I would look after him," Bucyk once said. "Sure, I said, no problem. I think it took only two weeks of training camp, and I was the kid and he was the guy in charge of the room. He was unbelievable."

Bucyk was an avuncular figure in the Bruins locker room in the early '70s. But he wasn't a mere figurehead. The guy could still play. When the 1970–71 Bruins won a franchise-record 57 games, Bucyk scored 51 goals and 116 points—both career bests by a long shot.

But it was the short shot that distinguished Bucyk. He specialized in top-shelf goals and put-backs from point-blank range. In a four-year stretch from 1971 through '74 he led the league in shooting percentage three times.

In the end John Bucyk was both an opportunist and a lifer. He logged more games for the Bruins (1,436) over more seasons (21) than any other player, and he scored more goals (545). He built a Hall of Fame career brick by brick. And he assumed nothing until the last brick was in place; when he entered the Hall in 1981, it was the first time he had ever set foot in the building. "I sort of made a promise I wouldn't pay a visit until I was in there myself," he said.

There was no doubt that he belonged. As the Bruins' longtime radio broadcaster, Bob Wilson, said during his induction speech, "With all of his Bruins' scoring records, the Chief had more milestones than the Trans-Canada Highway. But it is more important to say that Johnny Bucyk had more real friends—as contrasted to just plain fans—than just about any other professional athlete."

As long as Bucyk's playing career was, those years constitute barely a third of the time he's spent in the Bruins organization, including his time as a broadcaster and a member of the front office. June 10, 2017 marked his 60th anniversary with the team.

18

Kevin McHale
Celtics Power Forward, 1980–1993

There's irony in his notoriety. Today, the kind of flagrant foul Kevin McHale committed against Lakers forward Kurt Rambis in Game 4 of the 1984 NBA Finals would be considered selfish—a player giving in to emotion and risking ejection.

But in those days, as McHale later told Boston.com, the price "was just two free throws."

More to the point, McHale committed the foul not to settle a personal score, but to appease his teammates. Larry Bird had labeled the Celtics "sissies" after LA ran them off the floor in Game 3. In particular, Bird was pissed that Rambis went 7-for-7 from the paint.

Halfway through the third quarter in Game 4, LA was again fast-breaking at will. And, as McHale recalled, "M.L. Carr was yelling, 'Someone's got to go down! They're running us out!' After hearing that, I knocked [Rambis] down. And I said to M.L., 'You caused that.'"

That episode said much about the Celtics' unique chemistry in the 1980s. About the only thing they enjoyed more than winning was throwing each other under the bus afterward.

Kevin McHale had the perfect temperament for that team. During his 13 seasons in Boston he was both a sixth man and an iron man. He started just once in his rookie season under Bill Fitch, but contributed ten points a game for the 1981 NBA champions. "He never bitched once about how I used him," Fitch later said. "Even when he got really good."

By the time of the Rambis episode, in his fourth season, McHale was really good indeed, averaging 18.4 points and 7.4 rebounds per game. And he had yet to miss a game in his career. But he was still primarily a role player, albeit a highly effective one. His repertoire of low-post moves was unmatched. And if you hacked him, he killed you from the line (79.8% over his career).

The only thing that might have been harder than stopping McHale was scoring against him. "People don't remember what a really great defensive player he was," said Danny Ainge, who played with McHale for 7½ seasons.

How good could McHale have been if he had focused strictly on offense? He gave an indication at Boston Garden on March 3, 1985, when he set a Celtics record with 56 points against the Detroit Pistons. He hit 22-of-28 from the floor and 12-of-13 from the line. McHale was so hot, said Bird, "We should have thrown rocks at him for not going after 60."

He wasn't joking. On a team that elevated ball-busting to high art, Bird then delivered a masterwork. Just nine days later he scored 60 points—and exactly 60 points, the last two on a buzzer-beater—against the Atlanta Hawks to break McHale's record.

McHale laughed it off. "When you can't hold a record like that for ten days," he said, "this must be a pretty tough team to play on."

Tough enough that it wasn't until his sixth season that McHale shed his sixth-man role. But in his first year as a starter, 1985–86, the Celtics were merely one of the best basketball teams ever.

Statistically, McHale was even better the next year. But he broke a bone in his right foot near season's end. Against medical advice he played through the injury. And although he remained effective in the playoffs (21.1 points and 9.3 rebounds per game), he and his hobbled teammates (fellow starters Robert Parish Danny Ainge were also hurt) lost to LA in the NBA Finals.

Playing on a broken foot said a lot more about the kind of player Kevin McHale was than a hard foul he never wanted to commit in the first place.

Long after his playing career ended McHale continued to help his old Celtics teammates. As the Minnesota Timberwolves' vice president of basketball operations, he dealt Kevin Garnett to Boston in 2007.

17

Troy Brown
Patriots Receiver/Returner, 1993–2007

He's second on the Patriots' all-time receiving list, with 557 catches. He made 58 more in the postseason. That total included one of the most critical receptions in team history. It was good for 23 yards against the St. Louis Rams on February 3, 2002. And it moved the Patriots into Adam Vinatieri's field-goal range with 21 seconds left in Super Bowl XXXVI.

Yet, when Pats fans think of what made Troy Brown special, there's a good chance they'll picture him doing something other than catching a pass. They might think of him returning a punt 55 yards for a touchdown against Pittsburgh in the 2001 AFC Championship Game. Or recovering a blocked punt in the same game and lateraling to Antwan Harris, who took it 49 yards for another touchdown. To put it another way: Troy Brown's play on special teams contributed half of the Pats' 24 points in the game that got them to Super Bowl XXXVI in the first place. (And that was on top of his eight catches for 121 yards.)

Or maybe Pats fans picture Troy Brown making a tackle. But not one of the 14 tackles he made (along with three interceptions) while filling in at defensive back in 2004. No, he made the most important tackle of his career while playing offense.

It happened with 6½ minutes left in a 2006 AFC divisional round game at San Diego. The Patriots trailed 21–13. Chargers safety Marlon McCree had just delivered an icepick to the Patriots' hopes, intercepting Tom Brady at the San Diego 31.

Plenty of diva receivers would have simply thrown up their hands and pouted at that point. Instead, Brown immediately toggled to defensive mode. He pursued the play and stripped McCree during the return. Another Pats receiver, Reche Caldwell, recovered.

"The best play I've ever seen," said Brady, who cashed in the gift as the Patriots rallied to win 24–21.

Said Pats linebacker Tedy Bruschi, who made a game-saving defensive play or two in his career, "We needed the ball, we needed that conversion, and that's who [Troy] is."

That's who Brown was from the time he arrived in New England in 1993. Brown's coach at Marshall, Jim Donnan, advised Bill Parcells, New England's coach at the time, to draft him. Said Donnan, "Just watch him."

The Patriots took Brown in the eighth and final round, with the 198th overall pick. In a draft that featured No. 1 pick Drew Bledsoe, Brown was overlooked, even in New England. But what he lacked in pedigree, he made up for in desire and instincts. As Bill Belichick later said, "Nobody thought he could make the big plays—but all he did was make plays. He just kept making them."

Along with big plays, he did all the little things right. When he made that crucial catch in Super Bowl XXXVI, for example, the Patriots had no timeouts. But because Brown slipped an attempted tackle by Rams rookie safety Adam Archuleta at the 40, he was able to get out of bounds at the 36 and stop the clock. That left Tom Brady enough time to complete one last pass, to Jermaine Wiggins for six yards, before spiking the ball and leaving it to Adam Vinatieri to kick the 48-yard field goal that culminated the winning drive. It was a drive that pivoted not only Pats history, but also the fortunes of all of Boston sports in the new millennium.

Said Patriots owner Robert Kraft, "Troy Brown to me is the consummate Patriot, [with] what he did on the field, and the way he conducted himself off the field. He always put team first."

Brown carried that attitude into retirement. "I will always be a Patriot, just not in uniform," he said when he hung up his cleats in 2008. "We set the foundation for what this football team is about today—guys like Bruschi and Vrabel. We set the example of what it takes to be not just a New England Patriots football player, but what it means to be a champion."

16

Tom Heinsohn
Celtics Forward, 1956–1965

Maybe you know him only from his work as a color commentator on Celtics telecasts. If so, you might dismiss him as a blustering homer. In his world, every official has it in for the Green. ("These guys are *ridiculous!*") But to complain about Tom Heinsohn's lack of objectivity is to miss the *point* of Tom Heinsohn. It's not an act. He truly can't help himself. You don't spend nine years in a Celtics uniform, averaging 18.6 points and 8.8 boards per game, all the while becoming fully indoctrinated in the ways of Red Auerbach (who in some ways was Bill Belichick before Bill Belichick) and developing a deep-seated loyalty to the organization through all those trips to hostile arenas in places like Syracuse and Fort Wayne—and then throw all that aside in the interest of journalistic evenhandedness.

You can't do it. You can't forget nights like your coming-out party on March 5, 1957 at Kiel Auditorium in St. Louis. As a rookie you torched the Hawks for 41 points—and the Celtics lost, 104–102, on a phantom goaltending call against Bill Russell. (Auerbach was so mad he filed a protest—which came to nothing, of course.) Two years later, in the same building, same score, the refs *didn't* call goaltending when the Hawks' Bob Pettit swatted Bob Cousy's prospective game-tying buzzer-beater off the rim. Auerbach went ballistic again ("It was goaltending as flagrant as any I've ever seen"). And this time he had backup. "Tommy Heinsohn was right underneath," said Red, "and did he scream."

During that era of singular dominance (Heinsohn won eight titles in those nine grinding years), it was the Celtics vs. the field. Their shared sense of purpose forged a permanent bond. And Auerbach reinforced the *esprit de corps* by ensuring that everyone had a role. Cousy ran the point and dished out assists. Russell cleaned the boards and anchored the defense.

Heinsohn's job was to add reliable frontcourt scoring. No one ever took to the role with greater relish. (There's a reason he was nicknamed "Tommy Gun.") He shot without a conscience. Yeah, the results could be ugly—but when he was on, look out. Take the game against the Lakers on February 27, 1959, when Russell sat out with a sore right leg. Without their defensive stopper, the Celtics opted to turn up the offensive firepower. The result? A 173–139 blowout in which Boston set an NBA team record for points in a regulation game that still stands. Heinsohn, 18–of–28 from the floor, led all scorers with 43 points.

But Heinsohn wasn't just a sorer. He was a winner. He proved that in his rookie season. In the greatest NBA Finals Game 7 ever, the Celtics outlasted the Hawks 125–123 in double overtime at the Garden. And it wasn't the veterans like Cousy (2-of-20) or Bill Sharman (3-of-20) who carried the C's to their first title. It was a pair of rookies. Russell had 19 points and 32 rebounds. Banging under the boards, Heinsohn had 23 rebounds, and he led Boston with 37 points on 17-of-33 shooting.

So, yes, these days it's easy to roll your eyes when TV Tommy Heinsohn howls about a foul call. But when it's crunch time in a close game and he says the Celtics need to stop settling for the outside shot and take the ball to the basket, the man speaks from hard-earned experience.

In addition to his eight titles a player, Heinsohn added two more (1974, '76) as the Celtics' coach. He is one of just four people named to the Naismith Memorial Basketball Hall of Fame in both categories. Add four decades' worth of Celtics' broadcasts, and he's the only person to have been with the team for each of its 17 championships.

15

Cy Young
Red Sox Pitcher, 1901–1908

Start with this: He won 511 games. You could end with that, too. Sure, Cy Young pitched in the rag-arm era. But still: 511 wins.

Win No. 287 of Cy Young's career, on April 30, 1901, was also the first win in Red Sox history. And it was the first of many milestones that Young achieved during his eight years in Boston.

On October 1, 1903, he started the first-ever World Series game. On May 5, 1904, he pitched the first (and, so far, only) perfect game in franchise history. On June 30, 1908 he became the first pitcher to no-hit the Yankees (still called the Highlanders at the time). And more than a century later, his name is still sprinkled all over the Red Sox record book. He holds Sox single-season marks for starts (43), complete games (41), shutouts (ten, tied with Smoky Joe Wood), innings pitched (384.2), walks per nine innings (0.687), fewest home runs per nine innings (0.30, tied with Sad Sam Jones), and WAR (12.6). And he holds career records for wins (192, tied with Roger Clemens) and complete games (275).

Granted, the game has evolved so much that comparing pitchers who competed a century apart is essentially meaningless. So the most important thing that citizens of Red Sox Nation in the 21st century ought to know about Cy Young is this. His popularity, and his integrity, played a critical role in *founding* Red Sox Nation.

The American League was born of a players' revolt. When the National League had a monopoly, players had to accept whatever terms their teams dictated. The fledging American League gave them leverage. Some National Leaguers—such as Bill Dinneen, a 20-game winner with the Boston Beaneaters—used that leverage to squeeze better contracts from their current teams.

That pattern has played out repeatedly in the history of American sports. An upstart league drives up salaries. The established league matches them. The upstart league then folds. (Think: Donald Trump and the USFL.)

And in the nasty public relations war that the AL and NL waged in the winter of 1901, rumors soon swirled that the Boston Americans' prized signing, Cy Young, would follow Dinneen's lead and return to the National League, where he had pitched for 11 seasons.

Young put that rumor to rest with a letter to his new team: "Please pay no attention to any reports about my jumping my contract. I have signed with the Boston American League club for 1901, and I will play in that city or nowhere. I have no respect for a contract jumper. When I have given my word to a man or to a club the deal is closed."

True to his word, Denton True Young pitched for Boston's American League entry in 1901. And, at age 34, he surpassed expectations by winning 33 games. That helped the new team draw almost twice as many fans as the more established National League team in the South End.

Boston's upstart American Leaguers were in town to stay.

Like Babe Ruth, Cy Young held on a little too long, pitching until he was 44. Like Babe Ruth, he ended his career with a short stint with the Braves franchise. Like Babe Ruth he had mostly poor results (a 4-5 record) leavened with a last moment of glory—which, as in Ruth's case, happened in Pittsburgh. On September 22, 1911, Cy Young shut out the Pirates 1–0. He held out hope of pitching again the next spring: "Next to baseball I like to work along the furrows," he said from his Ohio farm, "but every time I take a little rest somebody circulates a report that I am down and out." But he never did appear in another major league game. He died in 1955, and the award that bears his name was instituted a year later.

14

Bob Cousy
Celtics Guard, 1951–1963

It was the most successful shotgun wedding in sports history. The flashy point guard from the local college basketball powerhouse—a team that had recently won an NCAA title and was a fixture in the national polls—was available in the NBA draft. The local NBA franchise, which had struggled through four losing seasons in its brief history and had meager attendance, had the first pick.

No-brainer, right? The Boston Celtics *had* to take Holy Cross star Bob Cousy. At the time, the Crusaders routinely outdrew the Celtics at Boston Garden, due largely to Cousy's ball-handling wizardry. "His passing antics were sufficient to send the huge crowd into choruses of oohs and ahhs," the *Globe*'s Bob Holbrook noted after Cousy led Holy Cross over St. Louis before a sold-out Garden crowd in January 1950.

So, three months later, with the top pick in the NBA draft, the Celtics naturally selected … Bowling Green center Charlie Share. New coach Red Auerbach minced no words in rationalizing the decision: "I don't give a darn for sentiment or names. That goes for Cousy or anybody else. A local yokel doesn't bring more than a dozen extra fans into your building. But a winning team does and that's what I aim to have."

Eventually Red ended up with both the local yokel *and* a winning team. But it took a roundabout journey to get there. Cousy signed with the Tri-Cities Blackhawks, who promptly dealt him to the Chicago Stags, who just as promptly folded. In a random disbursement draft, Celtics owner Walter Brown picked Cousy's name out of a hat.

That first large dose of leprechaun luck changed the Celtics' fortunes for good. Cousy proved to be both a drawing card and a winner. In his rookie season, attendance increased by almost 80% and the Celtics topped .500 for the first time. Cousy was an NBA All-Star that year, as he was in each of the 13 seasons he spent in Boston. The Celtics never had a losing record during that stretch, and they won six NBA titles, including five straight to close out Cousy's career.

Cousy didn't do it alone, of course. The Celtics didn't win their first title until Bill Russell arrived for the 1956–57 season (Cousy was named MVP, however). But like the consummate point guard that he was, Cousy set the table for all that subsequent success. Yes, he could score. He put up 50 in a four-overtime win over Syracuse in the 1953 NBA playoffs.

But more important, Cousy was a catalyst, leading the NBA in assists eight times and creating an atmosphere where team success trumped individual stats. (Despite those initial misgivings about his accidental point guard, Auerbach "gave me full rein," Cousy later said.)

His early detractors dismissed him as a "showboat," but Cousy displayed a winner's grit. In the 1957 NBA Finals, he led the Celtics with 31 points in a Game 4 victory over the Hawks despite having a tooth knocked out. And in the final game of his Celtics career, Cousy sprained his ankle after putting up 16 first-half points against the Lakers in Game 6 of the 1963 NBA Finals. He returned in the fourth quarter, and on a heavily taped ankle dished his final assist as a Celtic to help secure the game and another title.

Bob Cousy made it to Springfield (he was inducted into the Naismith Memorial Basketball Hall of Fame in 1971) but never left Worcester, where he helped make basketball palatable for New Englanders all those years ago. "Every jock gets up and tells the world how lucky he is," Cousy told Holy Cross Magazine *in 2009. "But I feel that I may be the luckiest one of all in terms of timing and being in the right place at the right moment."*

13

Ray Bourque
Bruins Defenseman, 1979–2000

It was a scene familiar to any Bostonian in the 21st century. Thousands of fans jammed City Hall Plaza to celebrate a championship. What made June 13, 2001 unique, however, was that the fans weren't celebrating a Boston championship. They were celebrating a Colorado Avalanche championship.

More accurately, they were celebrating Ray Bourque's first and only Stanley Cup. After just 15 months in Colorado, Bourque had accomplished something that had eluded him in 21 years in Boston. And Bruins fans wanted to let him know how happy they were for him.

The moment was simultaneously embarrassing and touching. It illustrated just how starved Bostonians were for a title celebration during a drought that stretched from 1986 to 2002. But it also showed just how much Boston fans appreciated Ray Bourque, who set a standard for dependability.

And Bourque returned that affection. "It is truly special to be a Bruin," Bourque told the City Hall Plaza crowd.

It was apparent that Bourque was a special Bruin almost from the day he arrived, in 1979. The Bruins' top draft pick was being compared to Bobby Orr. Said Brad Park, another renowned Bruins defenseman, "I can't remember when I've seen a more poised 18-year-old defenseman. He has all the tools. He can skate, shoot, pass the puck. ... He does everything with confidence; you can see it in the way he handles the puck, the way he passes it, and he has a nice low shot from the point."

It was a lot to live up to—but Ray Bourque did it. He won the Calder Trophy as the NHL's rookie of the year, appearing in every game and accumulating 65 points and a plus/minus of +52. In the playoffs he added 11 more points, second on the team. The Bruins advanced to the second round before falling to the Islanders, the eventual Stanley Cup champions.

That was the template for the next two decades. Ray Bourque showed up every year, every night. He played in at least 75% of the games during every Bruins season—1,518 in all. And he wasn't just putting in his time; he was a five-time Norris Trophy winner who made the NHL All-Star team in 16 consecutive seasons. He ended his career as the NHL leader in goals (410) and points (1,579) by a defenseman—and as the leader in shots on goal (6,206) among *all* players.

He also led the Bruins to the playoffs in all but one season during his time in Boston, although they could never close the deal. Bourque had the misfortune to play during a run of NHL dynasties, starting with the Islanders (four straight Stanley Cup titles, beginning in Bourque's rookie year) and continuing through Wayne Gretzky's Edmonton Oilers (five titles between 1984 and 1990) and Mario Lemieux's Pittsburgh Penguins (1991–92).

Twice Bourque led the Bruins to the Stanley Cup Final, in 1988 and 1990, both against Edmonton. They won just one game. "I tried to do my best," Bourque said after the Bruins were eliminated in five games in 1990. "I don't have my head down."

He summarized not only that season but also his entire tenure with the Bruins: "We got the best out of a lot of people in this room."

By winning it all in 2011, the Bruins assured that their fans would never again be reduced to celebrating a Stanley Cup by proxy. Better to remember Bourque for another emotional ceremony: the night of December 3, 1987, when the Bruins retired Phil Esposito's number. Bourque, of course, had been wearing that number—until he pulled off his No. 7 sweater and revealed his new number, 77, underneath. No other gesture demonstrated more clearly to Bruins fans that this guy got it.

12

Dave Cowens
Celtics Center, 1970–1980

His most impressive one-on-one battle played out not on the basketball court but in the pages of the *Boston Globe*.

February 1976. The undersized Celtics were scrapping toward their second NBA title in three years. Cowens, their 6'9" center, was their tallest player and unquestioned leader. He averaged 19 points and 16 rebounds per game and was, in Bob Ryan's words, "the single best basketball player in the world."

But Ryan, the *Globe*'s resident NBA expert, offered that appraisal in the context of calling Cowens out. In the third quarter of a game against Houston at Boston Garden, Cowens had committed a full-speed intentional foul on Rockets guard Mike Newlin in retaliation for Newlin's flopping to draw a charge.

"A brutal attack," Ryan called it. "Reprehensible and outrageous."

Cowens, as usual, didn't back down from the challenge. But he didn't get in Ryan's face in the locker room, the way so many other aggrieved athletes might have. Instead, he opted to play on Ryan's home court—by writing a rebuttal in the *Globe*. "Your opinions are noteworthy," Cowens wrote, "but this is an issue of principle."

And as far as Cowens was concerned, there was nothing more "reprehensible and outrageous" than the epidemic of flopping that had infected basketball at every level. "I have noticed that the number of pretenders has risen over the past three or four years," Cowens wrote. "This, in plain words, is what I call 'cheating.'"

So, in flattening Mike Newlin, Cowens was simply saying, *Enough*. "Pretending makes players think they can achieve their goal without putting in the work or effort that it takes to develop any skill or talent," he wrote.

In other words: Play the game right or suffer the consequences.

Dave Cowens played the game right. Although he was a Kentucky native, Cowens grew up a Celtics fan. And he came to town with the proper Celtics attitude. When Boston drafted him out of Florida State in 1970, he said, "I'd like to play forward, but I'll play wherever they want me to."

Good thing. Bill Russell had been gone for a year and Hank Finkel was obviously a stopgap solution at center. People assumed the same about Cowens when he took over the role. But a funny thing happened. "The Celtics keep winning with a 6'9" rookie midget in the middle," wrote the *Globe*'s Ray Fitzgerald. "This is against pro basketball law."

By then it was obvious that Cowens played by his own code, one that emphasized hustle and effort over everything else. In his third season he was named MVP as the Celtics won 68 games—more than any of the great Russell teams that preceded Cowens or Bird teams that followed. But they didn't win a title.

The Celtics finished the job the next season, beating the Bucks in seven games to win the 1974 NBA Finals. That Game 7 win came on the road. And with the Celtics' leading scorer, John Havlicek, struggling (6-of-20), Cowens stepped up with 28 points (13-of-25) and 14 rebounds in outplaying Kareem Abdul-Jabbar.

Two years later, the Celtics won it all again. Cowens averaged 20.5 points and 16.3 rebounds per game as the Celtics beat the Suns in six games (including an epic triple-overtime win in Game 5). And three months after the ugly Newlin episode, Bob Ryan praised Cowens as "the man whose spirit has made him synonymous with the entire concept of Boston Celticism."

Cowens' intensity took its toll. Suffering from burnout ("When you can't even get mad at the refs, something's wrong"), he took an unpaid leave of absence the following November. He returned after two months, but things were never the same. Even an old-school turn as player/coach in the 1978–79 season didn't help; that team finished 29–53. Still, the brilliance of Cowens' first six seasons remains undiminished. "I represent the working class of the NBA," he said just before his 1991 induction into the Naismith Memorial Basketball Hall of Fame.

11

Phil Esposito
Bruins Center, 1967–1975

As a Hall of Fame center, Milt Schmidt knew when to pull the trigger. He had the same gift when he became the Bruins GM. The first trade that Schmidt made, in May 1967, turned out to be the best in team history: Gilles Marotte, Pit Martin, and Jack Norris to the Blackhawks for Ken Hodge, Fred Stanfield—and Phil Esposito, a center with a left-handed shot. Like Milt Schmidt.

The deal required as much beginner's pluck as beginner's luck. Marotte was a promising defenseman who had raised fans' hopes. Not only that, there were reports that Esposito clashed with his coaches. Years later, Schmidt recalled his reaction: "I think I can put up with that problem."

Phil Esposito proved, indeed, to be a good problem to have. Before his arrival, the Bruins had missed the playoffs for eight straight years in a six-team league. His debut season in the spoked-B sweater started a run of 29 straight playoff appearances, including Stanley Cup championships in 1970 and '72.

It was a B.C./A.D. level of demarcation, and Bruins diehards embraced the change with biblical fervor. "Jesus saves," a famous bumper sticker read, "but Espo scores on the rebound."

That compliment was a back-hander. Esposito had a reputation for "garbage goals." Elsewhere, hockey purists might have sneered at the lack of grace in Esposito's game, but Boston fans loved it. "Scoring is easy," Esposito once said. "You simply stand in the slot, take your beating, and shoot the puck into the net."

Simple as that sounds, it was a revolutionary approach that borrowed principles from both retail sales (Location, location, location!) and wholesale (Volume, volume, volume!). And with the great Bobby Orr, among others, setting him up, Esposito cashed in at a record-setting rate. When he broke the NHL scoring mark of 97 points in a season on March 1, 1969, the Bruins still had 15 games left. He extended his scoring mark to 126 points—the equivalent of breaking Roger Maris's record by 18 home runs. And when Esposito set the single-season record for goals in 1971, with 76, he eclipsed Bobby Hull's mark by 18 goals. He scored those 76 goals on an incredible 550 shots on net, a record that still stands.

That 1970–71 Bruins team, the defending Stanley Cup champions, also set NHL records for wins (57) and points (121). The label "greatest team ever" was thrown around freely—and carelessly, it turned out. Montreal eliminated them in the first round of the Stanley Cup Playoffs. Afterward there were whispers that the big, bad Bruins had become too full of themselves—that stars like Orr and Esposito had played too many minutes in pursuit of records and had lost sight of the ultimate goal.

Esposito & Co. answered back the following season. Espo scored ten fewer goals, and had none in the six-game Stanley Cup Final against the Rangers. But he didn't care, because the Bruins won. "So I didn't score [goals]," he said afterward. "I was still a playmaker."

One of the best the Bruins ever had.

Esposito departed Boston the same way he arrived—via a blockbuster trade. The rebuilding Bruins dealt him to the Rangers in 1975. He never forgave team management. "I signed a contract in Boston for less money than I could have gotten from going to the WHA," he told the Toronto Star *in 2013. "And you know how they repaid me? Three weeks later, they traded me." Still, he's able to separate the bitterness he harbors for the organization from the bond he feels toward Bruins players and fans. With Ray Bourque's dramatic, classy gesture in 1987, when he switched from his assigned No. 7 to a new number, 77, the Bruins were finally able to raise Esposito's number to the rafters. Esposito said that mattered more to him than induction into the Hockey Hall of Fame "My biggest thrill was having my number retired at Boston Garden," he said. "That, to me, is where it's at."*

10

Carl Yastrzemski
Red Sox Leftfielder/First Baseman/DH, 1961–1983

If he didn't make Boston forget Ted Williams, he at least relegated Williams to a pleasant memory. In 1967 Carl Yastrzemski, longest link in a 50-year chain of Hall of Fame leftfielders at Fenway Park, produced a transformative season—a season instrumental in founding the modern Red Sox Nation.

Yastrzemski's performance leap was only slightly less astounding than the Red Sox'. Each year from 1961, when Yaz arrived, through 1966, Boston finished at least 19 games out of first. During that stretch Yastrzemski never had more than 20 homers or 94 RBI in a season.

His line for 1967: .326, 44 HR, 121 RBI. Good for the triple crown and MVP. (He also led the league in runs, hits, total bases, OBP, slugging, and OPS.) And the Sox, of course, achieved the Impossible Dream and won the pennant. They also won over Boston's jaded fans. After six straight years of attracting fewer than a million paying customers to Fenway, the Sox drew a record 1,727,832 in 1967. Attendance never dipped below a million again.

"Suddenly in 1967, we had the attitude of winners instead of losers," Yaz once said. "I think it changed the whole organization around."

Today, a spike in power numbers like the one Yaz had in '67 would raise eyebrows. But there was an innocent explanation: He'd spent his previous off-seasons taking classes at Merrimack College. With his courses complete, he devoted the entire '66 offseason to conditioning. His increased strength and stamina produced dramatic results—in more ways than one. Yaz hit in the clutch all season long. Yastrzemski's first homer of 1967 came in a one-run win over the Yankees. His last homer of 1967, a three-run shot in Game No. 161, was the difference in a 6–4 win over the Twins that lifted the Sox into a tie for first. That bomb was part of a 7-for-8, six RBI weekend with the pennant at stake.

Yaz had helped make the Red Sox relevant again, and he'd done it both in style and with style. Although he was just 5'11" and 175 pounds, he generated outsized power by holding the bat high and getting full rotation through his swing. (Go to YouTube and check out the follow-through on his 472-foot shot into the Fenway bleachers in 1977.) Add to that his outstanding defense; he played the Green Monster with the familiarity of a kid bouncing a tennis ball off his garage.

For most of his 23 seasons in Boston, Yastrzemski was more steady than spectacular. His lifetime average was .285, and he averaged 20 homers a year. But an entire generation took it for granted that Yaz would be in the lineup almost every night (only once did he play fewer than 100 games in a season) and in the All-Star Game almost every summer (his 18 ASG appearances is tied for fifth all time). Along the way he became the first American Leaguer to top both 400 home runs and 3,000 hits. And he reached the top of the Sox all-time list in 14 major offensive categories.

Through it all he played with the same intensity he'd had the first time he'd set foot in Fenway. "I'd go against anybody in a seven-game series having eight [other] Yastrzemskis out there," he once said. "I'd take my chances."

Like Ted Williams, Yastrzemski had a memorable Fenway farewell. But unlike Williams, who refused to acknowledge the fans after homering in his last at-bat, Yastrzemski made the fans the focal point. He didn't get to circle the bases, but he took a victory lap around the entire field before a sold-out, sobbing crowd at the conclusion of Yaz Day ceremonies on October 1, 1983—exactly 16 years after the Red Sox clinched the 1967 pennant. No, he never won a World Series, but Carl Yastrzemski still provided some thrilling October moments.

9

Eddie Shore
Bruins Defenseman, 1926–1940

He arrived in Boston in the fall of 1926 from the Edmonton Eskimos of the defunct Western Hockey League. That much is beyond dispute. But from there the Eddie Shore story sprouts lots of fuzz. "With Eddie, it has been almost impossible to separate truth from fiction," Stan Fischler wrote in a 1967 *Sports Illustrated* profile. "His bizarre behavior has been embellished in the stories about him, no doubt, but the stories have roots in truth."

A case in point: Shore's run-in with Billy Coutu, a veteran defenseman who joined the Bruins at the same time as Shore.

Coutu had a nasty reputation. (Within a year he would be banned from the NHL for life for assaulting a referee.) And he and Shore were both after the same starting job.

Shore, the story goes, grew up on a Saskatchewan ranch taming wild horses. At his very first Bruins practice, the story goes on, he challenged Coutu to a fight. Shore KO'd Coutu—but not before Coutu almost sheared one of Shore's ears off with (depending on which version of the story you read) a slash, a head butt, or a bite.

His ear dangling by a thread, Shore searched all over Boston until he found a doctor who would reattach the ear rather than amputate it. Shore refused anesthetic so he could supervise the procedure using a hand mirror. (Another version of the story says Shore pulled the stitches out and sewed the ear back on himself because he wasn't satisfied with the doctor's work.)

Do a little digging, and the facts start getting in the way of that story. Yes, Shore had a dust-up with Bill Coutu. But at didn't happen in his first practice. It happened on December 11, 1926, seven games into Shore's rookie season. As for that part about his ear—well, a contemporary *Boston Globe* account said only this: "Ten stitches were taken in Shore's head as a result of a hectic workout in which he and Billy Coutu bumped each other good and hard. Shore, one of the favorites of the Boston club, evidently has ousted Coutu from the regular berth on the defense."

Still, as Fischler said, the story had its roots in the truth. As a rookie, Eddie Shore went head-to-head with one of the NHL's toughest defenseman and won the starting job. He also won the adulation of Boston's hockey fans—and made the Bruins a viable commodity—with his damn-the-torpedoes style. "Most people of the day would skate down the side," the late Bruins legend Milt Schmidt once said. "But Eddie always went down the middle of the ice. People bounced off him like tenpins."

In his first season Shore helped lead the Bruins to their first Stanley Cup Final. (They lost to Ottawa.) In his second season Shore set what was then an NHL record with 165 penalty minutes—in just 43 games.

Eddie Shore became an eight-time All Star. He won the Hart Trophy as NHL MVP four times. Most important, he led the Bruins to their first two Stanley Cup titles, ten years apart.

One week after that second title, in 1939, the team held a victory dinner at Boston Garden. Coach Art Ross pointed at all the names etched on the Stanley Cup, which had already been around for almost 50 years at that point. Ross declared that the greatest of all those names was Eddie Shore—"And if I'm wrong on that, I'll take a bite of that Cup."

No one argued. In his day, Eddie Shore was the best there was—and that's no exaggeration.

Shore retired as an NHL player in 1940 because (he later told Fischler) he was suffering from cancer—which he claimed he cured on his own. He was inducted into the Hockey Hall of Fame in 1947. The movie Slap Shot paid homage to his colorful second act as owner of the Springfield Indians. ("Eddie Shore! Old-time hockey!") But despite his eccentricities and tight-fisted ways, said defenseman Kent Douglas, who played for Eddie in Springfield before becoming NHL Rookie of the Year at Toronto, "Studying under Shore was like getting your doctorate in hockey science."

8

Pedro Martinez
Red Sox Pitcher, 1998–2004

Most of Pedro Martinez's time in Boston was a frustrating squander. He was the best pitcher in baseball by far, but he was surrounded by too many Tomo Ohkas, Mark Portugals, Pete Schoureks, and John Wasdins. Pedro couldn't pitch the Red Sox out of their World Series purgatory all by himself. But, man, he *tried*.

1999 was peak Pedro. Just look at the stat line: 23–4 with a 2.07 ERA, 313 strikeouts, and a WAR of 9.7. (Aging Bret Saberhagen, at 10–6, was the only other pitcher on the '99 Red Sox to win more than eight games.) As eye-popping as those numbers look on paper, the way Pedro achieved them was even more impressive as it unspooled in real time—during the height of the steroids era. When Fenway hosted the '99 All-Star Game, for instance, Pedro struck out the first four National Leaguers he faced, including Sammy Sosa and Mark McGuire.

This from a Jheri-curled wisp who weighed less than an average high school pitcher.

The Red Sox sprinted away from the Oakland A's to win the AL wild card in 1999, almost singlehandedly because of Pedro. He closed the regular season with eight straight starts in which he had at least 11 strikeouts. He reached the pinnacle of peak Pedro in September at Yankee Stadium, racking up 17 strikeouts while allowing just one hit. This against a lineup that was on its way to a third World Series title in four years.

Pedro fanned eight of the last nine New York batters. Seven went down swinging. Had Chili Davis not guessed right and homered on a

1–1 fastball in the second inning, this would be in the running for the greatest major league game ever pitched.

In terms of pure pitching stuff, this was the best game of Pedro's best season. But in terms of the intangible stuff that separated Pedro from every other pitcher of that time, he turned in an even better performance a month later.

The American League Division Series between Boston and Cleveland was tied at two games apiece. Pedro had left Game 1 after four innings with a tweaked back. The Red Sox led 2–0 when he left; they lost 3–2. From there, the Sox and the equally pitching-challenged Indians made the ALDS look like a slow-pitch softball tournament. Cleveland won Game 2, 11–1. The Red Sox took games 3 and 4 at Fenway, 9–3 and 23–7. Back in Cleveland, the deciding game was 8–8 after 3½ innings.

That's when Pedro said *Enough*. He came out of the bullpen, balky back and all, and no-hit the Indians over the final six innings of a 12–8 Sox win. He then completed his season of seasons with another gem in Game 3 of the 1999 ALCS. Pedro threw seven shutout innings (and collected 12 strikeouts) as the Red Sox routed the Yankees (and turncoat Roger Clemens) 13–1.

That was Boston's only win of the series. As a further indignity, a New York writer (the *Post*'s George King) was one of two voters who left Pedro off the MVP ballot, robbing him of the award. (Jeremy Lehrman, author of *Baseball's Most Baffling MVP Ballots*, called this the worst snub ever.)

At the turn of the millennium, Pedro was about the only thing that kept Boston from meekly submitting to New York's dominance like the rest of the AL East. Red Sox Nation loved his defiance. ("Wake up the damn Bambino and have me face him. Maybe I'll drill him in the ass.")

The irony is that by the time the tide turned in the Boston–New York rivalry in 2004, Pedro had passed his peak and had all but waved the white flag. "What can I say?" he said after dropping two starts to New York in less than a week that September as the Red Sox were again relegated to wild-card status. "I just tip my hat and call the Yankees my daddy."

Pedro didn't give himself enough credit. All those fraught, four-hour games over the last six years were as tough for the Yankees as for him. (In his autobiography, Pedro noted that in every Red Sox–Yankees series during those years, "the fate of the free world rested upon the outcome … until the next one.")

The difference this time was that Pedro didn't have to beat the Yankees all by himself. "For years I had been asking the Red Sox for a little help, please," he wrote. "In 2004 the Red Sox came through. They got Curt Schilling."

The result? "Despite all the questions from Yankees fans about who my daddy was, the Red Sox had an answer that finally shut them up."

With his relentless competitiveness, Pedro Martinez played as big a part in the Great Shutting Up of 2004 as anyone else.

World Series ring in hand, Pedro moved on to free agency. The numbers he left behind (137–37, 2.52 ERA, 1,683 strikeouts, two Cy Young awards) made a solid case that he was the greatest pitcher in Red Sox history.

7

John Havlicek
Celtics Forward/Guard, 1962–1978

For all his scoring prowess, for all his heroics in the NBA Finals, for all his legendary stamina, John Havlicek achieved Boston sports immortality because of a single heads-up defensive play in Game 7 of the 1965 Eastern Division Finals.

Quick refresher. The Celtics led the Philadelphia 76ers 110–109 with five seconds left. Bill Russell attempted to inbound the ball under the Celtics basket, but the ball struck a guy wire overhead. Under the ground rules at the old Boston Garden, that resulted in a turnover. Philadelphia ball.

Now all the 76ers had to do was set up an inbounds play for a clean shot and a chance to win at the buzzer.

Philadelphia decided to use Wilt Chamberlain (30 points) as a decoy. Instead of looking for the big man, shooting guard Hal Greer would inbound the ball to forward Chet Walker, who would then feed it back to Greer for (the Sixers hoped) an open layup or a foul.

With his back to Greer, Havlicek scanned the floor. He knew Philadelphia had five seconds to get the ball in. He saw that Walker was open. So he counted in his head: *One thousand one, one thousand two, one thousand three…*

When he hit one thousand four, Havlicek sprinted toward Walker. And, as he later recalled, "I took a peak and I saw the ball midflight and I knew I could get a hand on it."

That's one way of putting it. Celtics radio announcer Johnny Most put it another way: *"Havlicek stole the ball!"*

It was a perfect John Wayne moment for a player who was, in fact, nicknamed for a character in a John Wayne movie: *Hondo.*

But when you widen the lens and look at the entirety of Havlicek's career, you realize that a more appropriate Hollywood nickname would be Zelig. Because for 16 years John Havlicek was on the scene for just about every big moment for the Boston Celtics.

He played every game as a rookie. He played every game in his final season. In between he played a total of 1,270 games, the most in franchise history. At his peak, he missed a total of four games in seven seasons. That included back-to-back seasons in which he averaged more than 45 minutes a game, tops in the league.

And it wasn't as if he just showed up. John Havlicek scored more than 1,000 points in each of his 16 seasons. His career total, 26,395, leads a franchise that has sent 28 players to the Naismith Memorial Basketball Hall of Fame (including Havlicek himself, who was inducted in 1984). He was a 13-time NBA All-Star and five-time member of the NBA all-defensive first team. He excelled as a sixth man, as a small forward, and as a shooting guard. In his best season, 1970–71, he averaged 9.0 rebounds and 7.5 assists per game, along with a career-high 28.9 points.

He played on eight championship teams and never lost a series in the NBA Finals. And he was instrumental in bringing every one of those eight banners home to Boston. As a rookie in 1963, he came off the bench in his second-ever playoff game to score 17 points on 8-of-14 shooting to help the Celtics get a key round-one road win over the Cincinnati Royals. The Celtics went on to win their fifth straight title and sixth overall in the Russell Era. By the time that era ended in 1969, Havlicek was a mainstay. He played every second of the Celtics' dramatic seven-game '69 Finals victory over the Lakers, averaging 28.3 points per game. (Sam Jones was second on the team at 18.7 points per game.) He also averaged 11.0 rebounds per game and 4.4 assists.

Five years later, when the Celtics made their next trip to the NBA Finals, Havlicek again led the team in scoring with 26.4 points per game in a seven-game victory over the Bucks. This included an NBA record nine points in overtime in Game 6. (A year earlier, Havlicek had set a franchise record by scoring 54 points in the playoff opener against the Hawks.)

And in 1976, Havlicek hit an off-balance 17-footer with :01 left in the second overtime of the Celtics triple-overtime win over the Suns in Game 5 of the NBA Finals, a contender for the title Best NBA Game Ever Played.

But if you play word association with any Boston sports fan, and you say *Havlicek*, the immediate response is "*...stole the ball!*"

Havlicek deflects credit as readily as he deflected Greer's pass. He attributed his success in part to good coaching: "Red Auerbach always said, 'Try to find an edge in whatever you're doing.' The only thing I could think of was counting [to five]."

And he credited Most for immortalizing the result. "Without Johnny this thing would never have happened," Havlicek said 50 years after his signature play. "It would have been an ordinary steal. Johnny parlayed it to legendary status."

Havlicek prefers not to be singled out, either for that play or for his many individual records. Instead, he sees himself as part of a continuum. "Once you're a Celtic you're always a Celtic," he told nba.com. "There's no other organization that's accomplished as much as the Celtics have. Bill Russell passed the torch to me and I passed it on to Dave Cowens."

6

David Ortiz
Red Sox DH, 2003–2016

When the designated hitter rule went into effect in 1973, the *Globe*'s Harold Kaese predicted it would initiate "a chorus line of slow, obese, decrepit, spavined, pot-bellied old men who can't get out of their own way but can still stand upright at the plate and make contact with the ball."

What baseball needed instead, wrote Kaese, was "more colorful performers, keener competition, and better publicity."

So it was a supreme irony that one of the most colorful, competitive, and PR-savvy performers in Boston sports history turned out to be a DH.

That it was David Ortiz was even more improbable.

Ortiz's first full season in the majors, with the Twins, was in 1998. Baseball was then in its "Chicks dig the long ball" height. America naively cheered on performance-enhanced Mark McGuire and Sammy Sosa as both obliterated Roger Maris's longstanding standard of 61 homers in a season. Ortiz, who hit just nine that year, was on no one's radar.

When he came to Boston in 2003, he had never hit more than 20 home runs in a season. No one foresaw that the next five years would bring an average of 42 homers and 128 RBI per season.

But the biggest number was two, as in the pair of World Series the Red Sox won in that stretch. The first, of course, came after the Red Sox made history by overcoming a 3–0 deficit to the Yankees in the 2004 ALCS. Ortiz delivered walk-off hits in each of the first two games of that comeback. This after dispatching the Angels with a walk-off homer in the ALDS.

So you could argue that in 2004 alone, Ortiz had three of the ten most memorable Red Sox postseason hits ever.

Ortiz set such a high bar that his greatest statistical performance in a postseason series has been largely forgotten. In the 2007 ALDS against the Angels, Ortiz reached base 11 times in 13 plate appearances, with five hits (including a pair of homers) and six walks. His average (.714), on-base percentage (.846), slugging percentage (1.571), and OPS (2.418) in that series were all career bests. But because the Sox swept the series, no single hit lodged in Boston's collective memory.

Compare that to what happened in the 2013 ALCS against Detroit. Ortiz was just 2-for-22 with one extra-base hit. But that lone extra-base hit was a game-tying grand slam in the eighth inning of Game 2. It changed the course of the series and became another iconic moment in Boston sports history.

Up to that point, Ortiz's most memorable moment of 2013 didn't even happen in a game. Instead, it came in a speech before an April 20 game against the Royals. Boston was still reeling in the aftermath of the Marathon bombing five days earlier. In a pregame ceremony, Ortiz stepped up to the mic and made a simple declaration that was both defiant and unifying. "This is our f---ing city," he declared, "and no one is going to dictate our freedom. Stay strong."

That set a tone in Boston for the rest of the year.

Ortiz cemented his reputation as both an inspiring leader and a clutch performer in the 2013 World Series. Again, his numbers looked like something out of Little League: .688/.760/1.188/1.948. But it was an impromptu dugout speech that became the enduring Big Papi Moment.

The Red Sox trailed 2–1 in the series and were tied 1–1 in the sixth inning of Game 4. Their offense was flailing, having managed a total of ten hits in Games 2 and 3. They had just two hits through five innings of Game 4 — and Ortiz had provided both. Rather than call his teammates out for their lack of support, Ortiz encouraged them to relax. "We better than this right here," he said. "Let's loosen up and play the game the way we do."

His words seemed to have little effect at first. Cardinals starter Lance Lynn got two quick outs. Then Dustin Pedroia stroked a first-pitch single to center. Ortiz was up next. Lynn, no fool, worked carefully, walking Ortiz on four pitches.

That brought up Sox leftfielder Jonny Gomes. He was the definition of a journeyman—the Red Sox were the sixth team he had played for in ten years. He was 0–for–9 so far in the series and was starting only because Shane Victorino was hurt. The Cards countered with reliever Seth Maness, who had yet to allow an earned run in the postseason. But he allowed one to Gomes, who launched a 2–2 sinker over the wall in left.

The Red Sox never trailed again in the 2013 World Series. They wrapped it up on the Fenway lawn in a cathartic celebration for the city of Boston.

So did Ortiz's dugout speech really make a difference? Gomes left no doubt. "It was like 24 kindergartners looking up at their teacher," he said later. "He got everyone's attention and we looked him right in the eyes, and that message was pretty powerful."

Although Ortiz is second to Ted Williams on the Red Sox' all-time home run list, and trails both Williams and leader Carl Yastrzemski on the team's all-time RBI list, he stands alone when it comes to clutch hits and indelible postseason moments.

5

Larry Bird
Celtics Forward, 1979–1992

H is arrival seemed scripted. It was 1979, and the once-proud Celtics had really let themselves go. For the first time since Red Auerbach had arrived in 1950, the team had endured back-to-back losing seasons. They needed a savior. They found one in rural Indiana, a mythical basketball hotbed. Even better, Auerbach acquired him using his legendary legerdemain. Red selected "the Hick from French Lick" a full year before the kid would enter the NBA draft.

Even better still, the Celtics found their savior the same year that the Lakers signed a savior of their own. And the two already had a history, having just squared off in an NCAA title game. Instant rivalry!

Boston could hardly wait for this new NBA era to begin. Bob Ryan: "The basketball fans of this city are in for what will be a decade or more of exquisite viewing pleasure."

Thanks to a relentless work ethic and simple, transparent values, Larry Bird not only lived up to the hype, but he actually surpassed it. "When somebody takes a chance on me like the Celtics did," he said, "I owe them something."

Whatever Bird owed Boston, he repaid many times over. He led the Celtics to an NBA championship in just his second season, in 1981. Two more titles followed, in 1984 and '86, during the most competitive and entertaining decade that the NBA—or at least the Eastern Conference—has ever known.

Bird brought swagger as well as skill. He was a rarity—a supremely confident player who loved to showcase his ability, but who ultimately put his team first. He knew he could score almost at will—and he proved it by putting up a franchise-record 60 points against the Hawks on March 12, 1985. It was just nine days after Kevin McHale had set the previous record with 56.

It was the ultimate Bird statement game. No one, including his teammates, was exempt from his competitive fire. He would dare an opponent to try to guard him, and then tell the other Celtics to get the hell out of his way.

And he always stood behind his legendary trash talk—even when things turned physical. "You can never back down," he said. "Once you do, people look at you different." He scuffled with everyone from lunch-bucket bangers (Marc Iavaroni, Bill Laimbeer) to kid-gloves legends (Julius Erving, Kareem Abdul-Jabaar).

But Bird preferred to get even with his shooting hand rather than his fist. He had 69 career triple-doubles (including playoff games) and four 50-point games. How many of those games were in response to perceived slights? That stat went unrecorded.

Still, a few examples were documented. Chicago, March 1987. Bulls coach Doug Collins had the effrontery to put a journeyman named "Gentle Ben" Poquette on Bird. Bird's verbal response? "Are you f---ing kidding me?" His physical response: 14 of the Celtics' first 16 points, en route to 33 by halftime. By then Collins had gotten the message and was throwing everyone, including Michael Jordan, at Bird to try to slow him down.

Given his fixation on getting even, you might think that Bird's most satisfying moment would have been the 1984 NBA championship against LA. That's when he finally got the better of his old rival, Magic Johnson. But during his Hall of Fame induction speech in 1998, Bird cited the 1981 title, over the Houston Rockets, instead. He gave a simple reason: "See, I had played a lot of basketball, but until I got to Boston I had never really won anything." So to finally win the final game of his season was, he said, "the most awesome feeling I've ever had in basketball."

After playing 13 years in Boston, Bird returned to Indiana and coached the Pacers for four years. He then became the team's president of basketball operations and completed a unique trifecta: MVP as a player (three times), Coach of the Year, and Executive of the Year. As his mother, Georgia, once told him, "For a blond-headed snotty ol' kid, you did very well."

4

Bobby Orr
Bruins Defenseman, 1966–1976

The correlation is clear. Between 1941 and 2011 the Bruins won the Stanley Cup just twice. Two titles in 70 years. Those two titles, in 1970 and '72, happened to bookend Bobby Orr's three consecutive MVP seasons. For all the talent those Big Bad Bruins teams had, they were able to win it all only during the narrow window when Orr was at his absolute best.

Boston was primed to love Bobby Orr from the moment he arrived in 1966. This was a hockey town even when the hockey was terrible. Playing in a six-team league in which the top four qualified for the post-season, the Bruins somehow missed the playoffs eight straight times. This stretch coincided almost exactly with the Celtics run of eight straight NBA championships—and yet the Bruins routinely drew bigger crowds at the Garden.

So you can imagine what the arrival of an 18-year-old prodigy—one that former Bruins GM Lynn Patrick predicted could be as big a star as Gordie Howe—did to gin up excitement. You can also imagine the level of excitement that resulted when the prodigy actually lived up to the hype. Bruins attendance increased 28% between 1966 and 1970 and has never really looked back.

Orr was a quicksilver skater who became the only defenseman ever to lead the NHL in scoring—and he did it twice (1970 and '75). He was almost solely responsible for Boston's hockey pinnacle. Said Bruins GM Harry Sinden, "There has never been a player like Bobby Orr in the history of the league. He's the finest player that's ever played."

His most famous moment was the "Flying Orr" goal on May 10,

1970, which completed a sweep of the St. Louis Blues and ended a 29-year Stanley Cup dry spell. But there were many other moments that were equally transcendent, even if they weren't frozen on film (or immortalized in Bronze; the Bruins unveiled a Flying Orr statue at TD Garden in 2010).

Orr's speed, and his ability to transition quickly from defense to offense, gave him a gambler's daring. In the clinching game of the 1972 Stanley Cup Final against the Rangers, Orr made a risky spin move in the face of an oncoming check as he retreated toward his own goal. It turned what had looked like a potential breakaway for New York into a scoring chance for Boston—and Orr cashed in what turned out to be the only goal the Bruins needed in a 3–0 win.

And it's not as if Orr's scoring prowess came at the expense of his defense. Bruins goalie Gerry Cheevers once said that Orr should win the Vezina Trophy because "Bobby has stopped more shots this year than any goalie in the league."

We'll leave it to another of Orr's teammates on those Stanley Cup-winning teams, Phil Esposito, to identify the definitive Bobby Orr moment. "Once when we were killing a penalty against the Oakland Seals, Bobby took the puck behind our net, tussled with one of their guys, and lost one of his gloves," Esposito says in the book *Hockey Talk* by Ross Bonander. "He went around by the blue line, came back, and picked up his glove. He still had the puck, killed well over a minute of that penalty—and then he scored. Greatest thing I ever saw."

Nagging knee injuries curtailed Orr's effectiveness and led eventually to what once would have been unthinkable: his departure via free agency to Chicago. He played only 36 games in three years for the Blackhawks before retiring. He was still just 31 years old when he was inducted into the Hockey Hall of Fame in 1979. He continued to revolutionize the game in retirement, as he helped expose the fraud that his former agent, Alan Eagleson, committed as head of the National Hockey League Players Association. Orr is still a familiar figure around Boston and remains one of the city's most beloved athletes.

3

Ted Williams
Red Sox Leftfielder, 1939–1942; 1946–1960

Any extended look at Ted Williams's career turns into a game of *What if?*

What if Williams hadn't played in an era when only the two league champions made the postseason? And what if his prime years hadn't overlapped with all those great Yankees teams of the mid-twentieth century? Four times Williams played on teams that won 93 or more games (in a 154-game season) but failed to win the pennant. So those teams stayed home. It's easy to imagine Williams leading at least one of those close-but-no-stogie Red Sox teams on a 2004 dirt-dogs-style run to a championship under a different playoff format.

And what if Williams had had a better relationship with the press? Could he have won more than two MVP awards?

No question. In 1941, Williams hit .406, the last time any major leaguer cracked .400. And he did so in style, refusing to sit out the season's final day with an average of .3996. That would have rounded up to .400. But, said Williams: "If I can't hit .400 all the way, I don't deserve it."

So he played both games of a doubleheader against the Athletics at Philadelphia's Shibe Park, collecting six hits in eight at-bats.

Sox manager Joe Cronin appreciated what Williams accomplished that afternoon. "If there's ever a ballplayer who deserved to hit .400," said Cronin, "it's Ted."

In addition to that .406 average, Williams led the league in seven other offensive categories that season, including on-base percentage—

an absurd .553. That's higher than any player in major league history other than the Barry Bonds action figure.

But the 1941 MVP award went to Joe DiMaggio.

OK, so the Yankee Clipper happened to have his record 56-game hitting streak that season, while playing centerfield for a pennant-winner. So maybe the MVP voters get a pass on that one.

But what about 1947? Again the voters picked DiMaggio over Williams—even though Williams won the triple crown. And if you think modern metrics provide a truer yardstick, fine. Williams had a 9.9 WAR in 1947 to DiMaggio's 4.8.

Nor did Williams win the MVP award in 1942, his other triple crown season. That time the winner was Yankees second baseman Joe Gordon—even though Williams put up better numbers in ten offensive categories.

And it's not as if the press even pretended that they weren't deliberately sticking it to Williams. When the 1942 MVP vote was announced, the *Boston Globe*'s Harold Kaese wrote, "Several times during the season you read on these pages that baseball's best hitter was making a poor popularity campaign."

Days later came news that Williams had been called to active military duty. He missed the next three seasons while serving in the Navy during World War II. And when the "police action" in Korea escalated into a three-year war, Williams was called to duty again.

Williams's military service leads to the greatest *What if?* of all. What if he hadn't missed almost five full seasons during his prime?

It's easy to extrapolate an answer. Some crunched numbers, based on the seasons that bracketed each of Williams's military stints, show that Williams lost approximately 766 hits, 561 walks, 569 runs, 150 home runs, and 450 RBI. Add those numbers to his career totals, and Williams jumps from 75th to eighth in hits, fourth to first in walks, 19th to first in runs, 19th to fifth in homers, and 14th to an extremely close second in RBI.

But so what? Those adjusted numbers just confirm what you already knew: Ted Williams was a phenomenal hitter.

But the thing that placed Williams on a higher plane in Boston sports history was, in fact, those five missed seasons. In World War II Williams served as a flight instructor. If that sounds like a skate, consider this: An estimated 15,000 airmen died in stateside crashes during World War II, many during training accidents.

And in Korea, Williams flew 39 combat missions. He took enemy fire on several occasions and ended one mission by belly-landing his burning plane. "Ted fit right in," said John Glenn, the future astronaut who served with Williams in Korea. "He was a Marine pilot, just like the rest of us, and did a great job."

Williams downplayed his contributions to the war effort. "Everybody tries to make a hero out of me over the Korean thing," he said later. "I was no hero. There were maybe 75 pilots in our two squadrons, and 99% of them did a better job than I did."

Whether that was false modesty or an accurate assessment of his flying skills is irrelevant. No matter how well Ted Williams did his duty, the fact is that he did it. *Twice.* And because of that he deserved to not only have his number 9 retired, but to also have a tunnel named after him.

Thirty-nine years after giving Williams a tepid sendoff, the Hub finally bid the kid adieu in style at the 1999 All-Star Game. A new generation of major-leaguers refused to clear the field, delaying the game by half an hour, to pay tribute to "the greatest hitter who ever lived." The ballpark shook with a sustained standing ovation during what proved to be Williams's final Fenway appearance.

2

Tom Brady
Patriots Quarterback, 2000–

"Football is so much about mental toughness," Tom Brady once said. "It's digging deep, it's doing whatever you need to do to help a team win. And that comes in a lot of shapes and forms."

Taking over from the face of the franchise at age 24 and leading the team to its first-ever Super Bowl win, for instance.

Or shaking off a poor start, including a pick-six, at age 39 to overcome a 25-point deficit and lead your team to its fifth Super Bowl win.

Suffice to say that no one in NFL history has shape-shifted more effectively than Tom Brady. His adaptability and his dependability are intertwined.

Brett Favre was a reckless gunslinger from the moment he arrived in the NFL until the day he left. When the Broncos won Super Bowl 50, they did so in spite of 39-year-old Peyton Manning, not because of him. Manning struggled to adjust to his diminished skills; his nine touchdown passes against 17 interceptions in his final season was by far the worst TD/INT ratio of his career.

At that same age, Brady threw the fewest interceptions of his career (2), versus 28 touchdowns, for the best TD/INT ratio in league history. And along the way he passed both Favre and Manning as the starting quarterback with the most wins in NFL history.

Not that any of that really mattered. As Brady has also said, in various ways and at various times, "The only thing I care about is this week."

Which is, of course, a variant of Bill Belichick's infamous "We're on to Cincinnati."

Inevitably, that leads to the silly, manufactured debate about whether Belichick made Brady or vice versa. The truth is, it's a perfect match. Belichick is a genius at exploiting an opponent's weaknesses with whatever tools he has available. But that approach works only if your quarterback is willing to adjust his style to accommodate the game plan. He also must be willing to stow his ego in his locker.

Brady has proven to be a master at both.

He's done it season by season. In 2004 he had just 474 pass attempts, his fewest for a full season, because he had Corey Dillon (345 rushes for a franchise record 1,635 yards) behind him. In 2015, when he basically had no one to hand the ball to over the final month (both Dion Lewis and LeGarrette Blount went down with injuries) he had the most pass attempts of his career, 624.

That's a difference of 150 pass attempts, based solely on what he had to work with. And in each case Brady played at a high level. The 2004 Pats won the Super Bowl; the 2015 Pats came within a failed two-point conversion of sending the AFC Championship Game into overtime.

Brady can also adjust game by game. In his 2014 Super Bowl run, Brady threw the ball 50 times each in victories over the Ravens and Seahawks. In between, he threw 15 fewer passes against the Colts because LeGarrette Blount steamrolled Indianapolis for 148 yards and three touchdowns. (Ironically, it was this game that hatched the Deflategate monster.)

Brady can even adjust from series to series. There was no better evidence of that than what happened at the end of Super Bowl XXXVI, the one that sparked the current golden age of Boston sports.

In the span of eight plays Brady morphed from the capable man-ager of a conservative game plan to the icy master of a high-risk two-minute drill. The Patriots and Rams were tied at 17. New England had the ball at their own 17 with just 1:21 left and no timeouts. To that point in his career Brady had made just 17 starts. To that point in the game he had completed just 11 passes, for a total of 92 yards. The numbers didn't inspire confidence.

But Brady did. Over the next 74 seconds, he hit J.R. Redmond for five yards (after stepping up in the pocket to avoid a sack); hit Redmond again for eight yards; spiked the ball to stop the clock; hit Redmond yet again for 11 yards; threw the ball away to avoid a sack; hit Troy Brown for 23 yards; hit Jermaine Wiggins for six yards; and spiked the ball to set up Adam Vinatieri's game-winning 48-yard field goal.

That alone would have cemented Brady's status as a Boston sports legend. But in the 15-plus years since then, Brady has won five more Super Bowls, the most of any quarterback in NFL history.

What other yardstick do you need to measure clutch?

In 2016 Brady surpassed even his absurdly high standards for "mental toughness," and "digging deep." His season began with a four-game suspension for Deflategate and ended with a record-setting Super Bowl performance (43-of-62 for 466 yards) as the Patriots overcame a 25-point deficit (another record) against the Falcons—all while Brady's mother, Galynn, underwent chemotherapy.

1

Bill Russell
Celtics Center, 1956–1969

Forget the 11 championships in 13 years. Forget the 10-0 record in Game 7s. Forget his numbers in those Game 7s (18.6 points and 29.3 rebounds a game). Forget that his first Game 7 victory, in double overtime, gave the Celtics their first NBA title. Forget that he was a raw rookie in that game—the tensest NBA Finals Game 7 ever played—but nevertheless put up 19 points and 32 rebounds. Forget that he also made a LeBron-like end-to-end sprint to block a shot in the closing seconds of regulation, a display of athleticism that Tom Heinsohn calls "the greatest play I ever saw in basketball."

Forget all that. Because as compelling as that evidence is, none of it is necessary to make the case that Bill Russell was the greatest gamer in Boston sports history.

Here's all you need to know: Bill Russell led the Celtics to eight straight championships.

Any counterarguments don't hold up. The most common is that there were only eight NBA teams when Russell started (14 when he finished) and fewer rounds of playoffs to endure. The implication being that, yeah, winning eight titles in a row was really kinda easy back then.

That's nonsense.

Yes, the vast expansion of all major American professional sports leagues, the added rounds of playoffs, and built-in equalizers like salary caps and free agency have made it difficult for any team since Russell's time to win even two championships in a row, let alone eight. But no team came close to winning eight straight championships *before*

Russell's time, either. Not the great Yankees teams of the early '50s, who just had to win the regular season title in an eight-team American League to reach the World Series. Not the great Canadiens teams of the late '50s, who played in a six-team NHL with two rounds of playoffs. Not the Canton/Cleveland Bulldogs of the 1920s, when the NFL had a 12-game season and *no* playoffs.

So much for the "That was a different era" argument.

And then there's this: Yes, the crop might have been smaller back then. But the cream of that crop was often just as good, comparatively speaking, as today's. Think of it this way: From 2015 through 2017 the two best teams in the NBA were clearly the Steph Curry Warriors and the LeBron James Cavaliers. It wouldn't have mattered if there were eight teams or 80, one round of playoffs or ten. Golden State and Cleveland were destined to meet in the Finals.

They split the first two series before Golden State won the third by bagging Kevin Durant.

It's laughable to think that ether of those teams could have beaten the other five straight times in the NBA Finals.

But that's basically what the Celtics accomplished with Bill Russell. Of those eight straight titles, five came against the Lakers (two came against the Hawks, one against the Warriors). And those Lakers teams got tougher as the decade went along. Boston's eighth straight championship, in 1966, came against a Lakers roster that included three future Hall of Famers: Jerry West, Elgin Baylor, and Gail Goodrich. LA pushed the Celtics to seven games but still couldn't overtake them. Why? "Russell was the difference again," said Lakers coach Fred Schaus.

Bill Russell could have retired after the 1966 NBA Finals with his legacy as Boston's ultimate winner secured. But he tacked on a remarkable coda.

It started with a great humbling.

After the 1966 season Red Auerbach retired as Celtics coach and appointed Russell his successor—and Russell would also continue to play. No pressure: Russell was merely the first African-American head coach of a major professional sports team, during the racially charged 1960s. And he was expected to continue the Celtics' eight-year run as champions while serving as player/coach.

Instead, the streak ended with a thud. The 76ers finished eight games ahead of the Celtics in the regular season, and then beat them in the Eastern Division Finals four games to one. Game five was a 140-116 demolition. Russell's longtime rival, Wilt Chamberlain, outscored Russell 29–4 in that game and went on to win the NBA title that Russell and the Celtics had denied him for so long.

A less confident man might have slinked away after that. Not Russell.

Although the Celtics struggled to a pedestrian fourth-place finish in 1968, they avenged their loss to the 76ers in the Eastern Division Finals. Then they beat the Lakers for the title *again*.

Boston and LA met yet again in the 1969 NBA Finals. This time the Lakers had Wilt Chamberlain. They also had home court advantage.

The Celtics and their 35-year-old player/coach dropped the first two games. But they rallied to push the series to the limit. And they won Game 7 on the road. "I honestly didn't think it could be done," Russell said afterward. "But here we are with another flag."

After that game, Bill Russell walked away. No Celtics player—or coach—has won back-to-back NBA titles since. To say nothing of eight in a row.

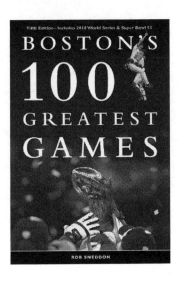

ALSO BY ROB SNEDDON

BOSTON'S 100 GREATEST GAMES
Fifth Edition – Includes 2018 World Series & Super Bowl 53

This provocative book ranks Boston's 100 greatest games of all time, across all sports. The bloody sock. A Harvard tie. Fisk's pole dance. Orr's swan dive. Havlicek's steal. Butler's pick. And of course the Patriots' epic comeback in Super Bowl 51. Relive all the landmark events you remember plus many you forgot—and discover some you never knew about.

2018, Candlepin Press, Available on Amazon.com

THE PHANTOM PUNCH
The Story Behind Boxing's Most Controversial Bout

2016, Rowman & Littlefield, Available on Amazon.com

Made in the USA
Columbia, SC
22 December 2020

29735513R00136